It's another great book from CGP...

Computer programming is great fun. Fact.
But AQA's new GCSE Computer Science exams are a pretty serious business
— to do well, you'll really need to know your ALU from your OMG.

That's where this CGP book comes in. We explain each topic in just the right
level of depth — including programming in AQA's set languages. Exciting!

What's more, there's plenty of advice for the trickiest parts and tips for
doing well in the exams. You could say it's... array of sunshine.

How to access your free Online Edition

This book includes a free Online Edition to read on your PC, Mac or tablet.
To access it, just go to **cgpbooks.co.uk/extras** and enter this code...

1111 8174 5888 0554

By the way, this code only works for one person. If somebody else has used
this book before you, they might have already claimed the Online Edition.

CGP — still the best! ☺

Our sole aim here at CGP is to produce the highest quality books —
carefully written, immaculately presented and dangerously close to being funny.

Then we work our socks off to get them out to you
— at the cheapest possible prices.

Contents

Published by CGP

Based on the classic CGP style created by Richard Parsons.

Editors: Martha Bozic, Sammy El-Bahrawy, Shaun Harrogate and Michael Weynberg.

Contributor: Shaun Whorton

Proofreaders: Neil Hastings and Simon Little.

ISBN: 978 1 78908 609 6

With thanks to Emily Smith for the copyright research.

Android is a trademark of Google Inc.

This book is an independent publication and is neither affiliated with, nor authorized, sponsored, or approved by, Microsoft Corporation.

Printed by Elanders Ltd, Newcastle upon Tyne.
Clipart from Corel®

You will sit <u>two exam papers</u> at the end of your AQA GCSE Computer Science course. <u>Paper 1</u> will cover the content in <u>sections 1-3</u> and <u>Paper 2</u> will cover the content in <u>sections 4-7</u>, though <u>both</u> papers may have questions that <u>assume knowledge</u> from <u>any section</u> in the book.

Computational Thinking

Computational thinking is all about the steps you take to find the best solution to a complex problem.
To be honest, your decision to buy this revision guide shows that you're already a great computational thinker.

Three Key Techniques for Computational Thinking

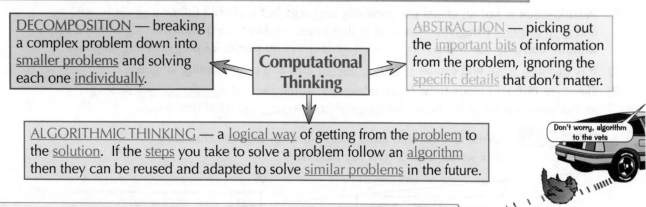

DECOMPOSITION — breaking a complex problem down into smaller problems and solving each one individually.

Computational Thinking

ABSTRACTION — picking out the important bits of information from the problem, ignoring the specific details that don't matter.

ALGORITHMIC THINKING — a logical way of getting from the problem to the solution. If the steps you take to solve a problem follow an algorithm then they can be reused and adapted to solve similar problems in the future.

Don't worry, algorithm to the vets

These techniques are all used in Real-Life...

Computational thinking is something you'll do all the time without even noticing.

For example, when deciding which film to watch at the cinema with your family:

Decomposition	Abstraction	
Things to look at	Details to ignore	Details to focus on
What type of films are on?	Plot details, actors and director.	Film genre and age rating.
What times are the films on?	Days other than the date you're going.	Start and end times on the date you're going.
What are the reviews like?	In depth analysis of the characters and plot.	Ratings

Algorithmic thinking may involve coming up with some logical steps to reach a decision.
E.g. listing all of the films that are showing, then deleting all the age restricted films and ones with poor ratings.
Getting each family member to vote for their favourite, then picking the film with the most votes.

If the family went to see a film the following week they could use the same processes of decomposition, abstraction and algorithmic thinking, but they would have to do the research and make the decisions again.

... and the Same Skills can be used in Computer Science

Computer scientists rely on decomposition, abstraction and algorithmic thinking to help them turn a complex problem into small problems that a computer can help them to solve.

See p5-6 for more on sorting algorithms.

Imagine the task is to sort a list of product names into alphabetical order:

* One part of the decomposition might decide what alphabetical order means — letters are straightforward but what if some entries in the list contain numbers and punctuation?

* Another part of the decomposition might look at comparing the entries — this could be decomposed further into how you could compare two entries, three entries, etc.

* Abstraction will help the programmer focus on the important bits — it doesn't matter what the entries are and what they mean. The important information is the order of the characters in each entry.

* Algorithmic thinking will put the tasks into a step by step process. For example, you might compare the first two entries and order them, then compare the third entry to each of the first two and put it in the correct place, then compare the fourth entry to each of the first three, etc.

I wasn't picking my nose, I was just doing a bit of abstraction...

Decomposition and abstraction are important skills that you'll need to develop if you want to succeed in your exams. You should be able to take a problem, break it down into small manageable tasks and ignore all of the details that don't matter. Try out your skills whenever you have a real-life decision to make.

Writing Algorithms — Pseudo-code

Algorithms are just sets of <u>instructions</u> for solving a problem. In real-life they can take the forms of recipes, assembly instructions, directions, etc. but in computer science they are often written in pseudo-code.

Algorithms can be written using *Pseudo-code*

1) Pseudo-code is not an actual programming language but it should follow a <u>similar structure</u> and <u>read like one</u> (roughly). The idea is that pseudo-code clearly shows an algorithm's steps without worrying about the <u>finer details</u> (syntax) of any particular programming language.

2) It is <u>quick to write</u> and can be <u>easily converted</u> into any programming language.

3) There are different ways to write pseudo-code — they are all <u>equally correct</u> as long as the person reading the code can <u>follow it</u> and <u>understand</u> what you mean.

EXAMPLE: Write an algorithm using pseudo-code to calculate the salary of a worker after a 10% pay increase.

A <u>simple solution</u> to the problem would be:

```
Take worker's current salary
Multiply the salary by 1.1
Display the answer
```

This solution is perfectly adequate as the problem has been <u>split down</u> into steps and it is <u>obvious</u> to the reader what to do at <u>each stage</u>.

A more <u>useful solution</u> is shown here:

```
salary ← USERINPUT
newsalary ← salary * 1.1
OUTPUT newsalary
```

This solution is better as the <u>words</u> and <u>structure</u> resemble a real <u>programming language</u>. It can be more <u>easily adapted</u> into real code.

Make sure your pseudo-code isn't *Too Vague*

Even though pseudo-code isn't a formal <u>programming language</u> you still need to make sure it's <u>readable</u>, <u>easy to interpret</u> and not too <u>vague</u>.

P.E.A. Fingers up Ma'am You're coming with me.

EXAMPLE: When registering on a website, a user's password should be more than 6 characters long and it must be different from their username. Write an algorithm to check if the password is valid. If it's invalid it should say why.

```
IF the length of the password is less than or equal
to 6 characters long OR password is the same as the
username THEN it is invalid ELSE the password is valid
```

This code is <u>too vague</u> and <u>unstructured</u>. It won't give reasons why the password is invalid and doesn't show the <u>inputs</u> and <u>outputs</u> (see p12).

The pseudo-code asks the user to <u>input</u> a username and password and stores them as <u>variables</u>.

The code gives <u>different outputs</u> depending on why the password is <u>invalid</u>.

Notice that the <u>indentation</u> of the pseudo-code makes it more <u>readable</u>.

```
username ← USERINPUT
password ← USERINPUT
IF length of password ≤ 6 THEN
    OUTPUT 'Password is too short.'
ELSE
    IF password = username THEN
    OUTPUT 'Password is the same as username.'
    ELSE
        OUTPUT 'Password is valid.'
    ENDIF
ENDIF
```

The first IF statement checks to see if the password is <u>too short</u> and the second checks if it's <u>the same as the username</u>.

See p12 for more on IF statements.

Pseudo-code isn't always everything it appears to be...

An algorithm is not the same thing as a computer program. A computer program is just one possible implementation of the algorithm — there are often many different ways to implement the same algorithm.

Writing Algorithms — Flowcharts

Algorithms can also be shown using a flowchart, and just like for pseudo-code, there are different ways to write the same algorithm. You do get to draw some different shapes though, so things are looking up.

Flowcharts use Different Boxes for different Commands

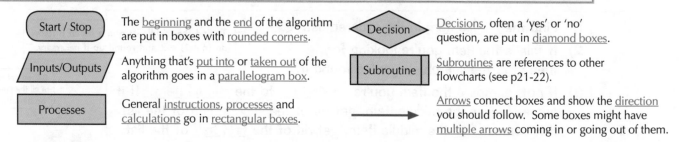

Start / Stop — The beginning and the end of the algorithm are put in boxes with rounded corners.

Inputs/Outputs — Anything that's put into or taken out of the algorithm goes in a parallelogram box.

Processes — General instructions, processes and calculations go in rectangular boxes.

Decision — Decisions, often a 'yes' or 'no' question, are put in diamond boxes.

Subroutine — Subroutines are references to other flowcharts (see p21-22).

Arrows connect boxes and show the direction you should follow. Some boxes might have multiple arrows coming in or going out of them.

Algorithms can be written as Flowcharts

Flowcharts can show sequence, selection, iteration or a combination of them.

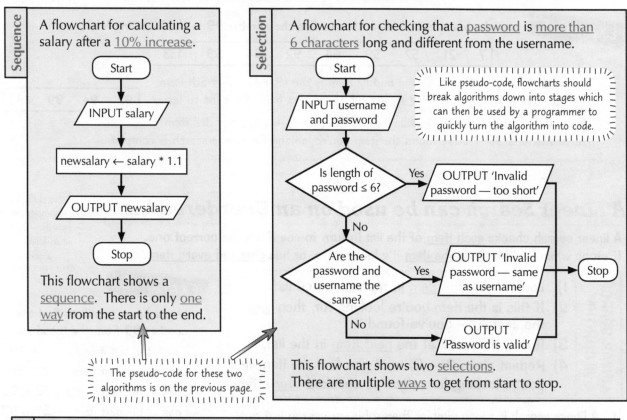

Sequence

A flowchart for calculating a salary after a 10% increase.

Start → INPUT salary → newsalary ← salary * 1.1 → OUTPUT newsalary → Stop

This flowchart shows a sequence. There is only one way from the start to the end.

The pseudo-code for these two algorithms is on the previous page.

Selection

A flowchart for checking that a password is more than 6 characters long and different from the username.

Start → INPUT username and password → Is length of password ≤ 6? — Yes → OUTPUT 'Invalid password — too short'

No → Are the password and username the same? — Yes → OUTPUT 'Invalid password — same as username' → Stop

No → OUTPUT 'Password is valid'

Like pseudo-code, flowcharts should break algorithms down into stages which can then be used by a programmer to quickly turn the algorithm into code.

This flowchart shows two selections. There are multiple ways to get from start to stop.

Iteration

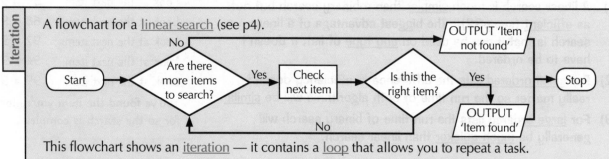

A flowchart for a linear search (see p4).

Start → Are there more items to search? — No → OUTPUT 'Item not found' → Stop

Yes → Check next item → Is this the right item? — Yes → OUTPUT 'Item found' → Stop

No → (loop back to Are there more items to search?)

This flowchart shows an iteration — it contains a loop that allows you to repeat a task.

Check out my flow, as the words just go, to and fro, yo...

Flowcharts should show the general flow of an algorithm without going into too much detail at each step. When you're making your own flowchart, make sure that all paths lead to the end. My best friend once got stuck in a flowchart — he got caught up in an infinite loop and was never seen again...

Search Algorithms

Computers need to follow search algorithms to find items in a list — the ones you'll need to know about are binary search and linear search. Now, if only someone could make a search algorithm to find my keys.

A Binary Search looks for items in an Ordered List

BINARY SEARCH ALGORITHM

1) Find the <u>middle item</u> in the ordered list.

2) If this is the item you're looking for, then <u>stop</u> the search — you've found it.

3) If not, <u>compare</u> the item you're <u>looking for</u> to the <u>middle item</u>. If it comes <u>before</u> the middle item, get rid of the <u>second half</u> of the list. If it comes <u>after</u> the middle item, get rid of the <u>first half</u> of the list.

4) You'll be left with a list that is <u>half the size</u> of the original list. Repeat steps 1) – 3) on this <u>smaller list</u> to get an even smaller one. Keep going until you find the item you're looking for.

> To find the <u>middle item</u> in a list of n items do (n + 1) ÷ 2 and round up if necessary.

OK, so get rid of all the teeth on the left...

EXAMPLE: Use the binary search algorithm to find the number 99 in the following list.

| 7 | 21 | 52 | 59 | 68 | 92 | 94 | 99 | 133 |

There are 9 items in the list so the middle item is the (9 + 1) ÷ 2 = 5th item.
The 5th item is 68 and 68 < <u>99</u> so get rid of the first half of the list to leave:

| 92 | 94 | 99 | 133 |

There are 4 items left so the middle item is the (4 + 1) ÷ 2 = 2.5 = 3rd item
The 3rd item is 99. You've found the item you're looking for so the search is complete.

A Linear Search can be used on an Unordered List

A linear search checks <u>each item</u> of the list in turn to see if it's the correct one. It stops when it either <u>finds the item</u> it's looking for, or has <u>checked every item</u>.

> It's important that you show <u>every step</u> when following these algorithms.

LINEAR SEARCH ALGORITHM

1) Look at the <u>first item</u> in the unordered list.

2) If this is the item you're looking for, then <u>stop</u> the search — you've found it.

3) If not, then look at the <u>next item</u> in the list.

4) Repeat steps 2) – 3) until you find the item that you're looking for or you've checked <u>every item</u>.

1) A linear search is much <u>simpler</u> than a binary search but not as <u>efficient</u> (see p32). The biggest advantage of a linear search is that it can be used on <u>any type</u> of list, it doesn't have to be ordered.

2) For <u>small ordered lists</u> the difference in efficiency doesn't really matter so the run time of both algorithms will be <u>similar</u>.

3) For <u>large ordered lists</u> the run time of binary search will generally be <u>much quicker</u> than linear search.

EXAMPLE:

Use a linear search to find the number 99 from the list above.

Check the first item:	7 ≠ 99
Look at the next item:	21 ≠ 99
Look at the next item:	52 ≠ 99
Look at the next item:	59 ≠ 99
Look at the next item:	68 ≠ 99
Look at the next item:	92 ≠ 99
Look at the next item:	94 ≠ 99
Look at the next item:	99 = 99

You've found the item you're looking for so the search is complete.

And my search for the perfect chocolate sundae continues...

Search algorithms might seem like a bit of a faff for you to follow when you can just look at a list and pick out the item you want straight away. Sadly, computers can only compare two numbers at a time, so they need to follow algorithms like these to find what they're looking for. When you're following these search algorithms, always follow every step exactly as a computer would and don't go skipping ahead.

Sorting Algorithms

I'm sure you all know how to sort things into numerical or alphabetical order but try telling a computer that. You'll need to be able to follow and carry out the two sorting algorithms on the next two pages.

A Bubble Sort compares Pairs of items

The bubble sort algorithm is used to sort an unordered list of items.
The algorithm is very simple to follow but can often take a while to actually sort a list.

BUBBLE SORT ALGORITHM	
	1) Look at the first two items in the list.
	2) If they're in the right order, you don't have to do anything. If they're in the wrong order, swap them.
	3) Move on to the next pair of items (the 2nd and 3rd entries) and repeat step 2).
	4) Repeat step 3) until you get to the end of the list — this is called one pass. The last item will now be in the correct place, so don't include it in the next pass.
	5) Repeat steps 1) – 4) until there are no swaps in a pass.

Each pass will have one less comparison than the one before it.

EXAMPLE:

Use the bubble sort algorithm to write these numbers in ascending order.

66	21	38	15	89	49

First pass:

66	21	38	15	89	49	Compare 66 and 21 — swap them.
21	66	38	15	89	49	Compare 66 and 38 — swap them.
21	38	66	15	89	49	Compare 66 and 15 — swap them.
21	38	15	66	89	49	Compare 66 and 89 — no swap.
21	38	15	66	89	49	Compare 89 and 49 — swap them.
21	38	15	66	49	89	End of first pass.

After the 2nd pass the order of the numbers will be: 21 15 38 49 66 89
After the 3rd pass the order of the numbers will be: 15 21 38 49 66 89
There are no swaps in the 4th pass so the list has been sorted: 15 21 38 49 66 89

The bubble sort is considered to be one of the simplest sorting algorithms as it only ever focuses on two items rather than the whole list of items.

Pros
- It's a simple algorithm that can be easily implemented on a computer.
- It's an efficient way to check if a list is already in order. For a list of n items you only have to do one pass of n – 1 comparisons to check if the list is ordered or not.
- Doesn't use very much memory as all the sorting is done using the original list.

Cons
- It's an inefficient way to sort a list — for a list of n items, the worst case scenario would involve you doing $\frac{n(n-1)}{2}$ comparisons.
- Due to being inefficient, the bubble sort algorithm is pretty slow for very large lists of items.

Use a bubble sort to order this list (greatest first):

Newcastle, Liverpool, Blackpool, Chelsea, Barcelona, Stevenage Reserves, Sunderland

But Miss, the teams are already sorted.

My friend's always happy, you know the type, the bubbly sort...

When following an algorithm there are no shortcuts, just follow the instructions from start to finish. A common mistake is to forget the final pass because you realise that the list is already in order, remember that you should always show a pass when nothing changes to complete the algorithm as a computer would.

Sorting Algorithms

The other sorting algorithm you'll need to learn is the merge sort — it splits a list apart and then magically merges it back together in the correct order. I really hope you're ready to see something special.

A Merge Sort Splits the list apart then Merges it back together

The merge sort algorithm is an example of a <u>divide-and-conquer</u> algorithm and takes advantage of two facts:

* Small lists are <u>easier to sort</u> than large lists.
* It's easier to merge <u>two ordered lists</u> than two unordered lists.

MERGE SORT ALGORITHM	
1)	<u>Split</u> the list in <u>half</u> (the smaller lists are called <u>sub-lists</u>) — the second sub-list should start at the <u>middle item</u> (see p4).
2)	Keep repeating step 1) on each sub-list until <u>all the lists</u> only contain <u>one item</u>.
3)	<u>Merge pairs</u> of sub-lists so that each sub-list has twice as many items. Each time you merge sub-lists, <u>sort the items</u> into the right order.
4)	Repeat step 3) until you've merged <u>all the sub-lists</u> together.

EXAMPLE: Use the merge sort algorithm to write these letters in alphabetical order.

1) <u>Split</u> the original list of 8 items into <u>two lists</u>, the second list should start at the $(8 + 1) \div 2 = 4.5 = $ <u>5th item</u>.

2) Carry on <u>splitting</u> the sub-lists until each list only has <u>one item</u> in it.

3) <u>Merge</u> and <u>order</u> sub-lists back together. Note that merging is always performed on <u>two ordered lists</u> and is <u>very simple</u> to do. E.g.

> Compare <u>F</u> and <u>A</u> — <u>move A</u> to the new list.
> Compare <u>F</u> and <u>L</u> — <u>move F</u> to the new list.
> Compare <u>P</u> and <u>L</u> — <u>move L</u> to the new list.
> <u>P</u> is the <u>last item</u> in the new list.

4) Keep <u>merging</u> sub-lists until you only have <u>one list</u>.

You'll often be unable to <u>split</u> or <u>merge</u> lists <u>evenly</u>. For example, sometimes you'll have to merge a list containing <u>two items</u> with a list containing <u>one item</u> to make a list of <u>three items</u>.

Pros	Cons
• In general, it's much <u>more efficient</u> and <u>quicker</u> than the bubble sort algorithm (p5) for <u>large lists</u>, and has a <u>similar running time</u> for <u>short lists</u>. • It has a very <u>consistent running time</u> regardless of how ordered the items in the original list are.	• Even if the list is <u>already sorted</u>, it still goes through the whole <u>splitting</u> and <u>merging</u> process, so a bubble sort may be <u>quicker</u> in some cases. • It uses <u>more memory</u> than the bubble sort because it has to create additional lists.

Due to its efficiency, the merge sort algorithm (or variations of it) are used in many programming languages such as Java™, Python® and Perl as the primary sorting algorithm.

Merging a visit to my grandma's with a paintball trip went badly...

When doing a merge sort it's important process — if you only show the merging I think the key thing that we can all take that you show the splitting process <u>and</u> the merging process then you've only shown half the algorithm. from this page is to never merge-sort your pets.

Revision Questions for Section One

Well that's <u>algorithms</u> all <u>done</u> and <u>dusted</u>. Or so you thought — just wait until you start <u>Section Two</u>.
- Try these questions and <u>tick off each one</u> when you <u>get it right</u>.
- When you've done <u>all the questions</u> for a topic and are <u>completely happy</u> with it, tick off the topic.

Computational Thinking (p1) ☑

1) What is meant by: a) decomposition?   b) abstraction? ☑
2) Why is using algorithmic thinking useful when solving a problem? ☑
3) Outline the decomposition, abstraction and algorithmic processes for choosing a film at the cinema. ☑

Pseudo-code and Flowcharts (p2-3) ☑

4) What is pseudo-code? Give three features of well-written pseudo-code. ☑
5) What are the benefits of writing algorithms in pseudo-code rather than a programming language? ☑
6) Draw the five box types used on flowcharts and say what each one is used for. ☑
7) What do sequences, selections and iterations look like on a flowchart? ☑
8)* Draw a flowchart to check if a new username is valid. Usernames should be at least
   5 characters long and unique. If it's invalid, the algorithm should give the reason why
   and get the user to enter another username. ☑

Search Algorithms (p4) ☑

9) What are the four steps of the binary search algorithm? ☑
10) What are the four steps of a linear search algorithm? ☑
11)* Here's a fascinating list of British towns and cities:

   Ashington, Brecon, Chester, Dagenham, Morpeth, Usk, Watford

   a) Use a binary search to find "Morpeth" in this list:
   b) Now do the same using a linear search. ☑
12) What are the benefits and drawbacks of using a linear search over a binary search? ☑

Sorting Algorithms (p5-6) ☑

13) a) What are the five steps of the bubble sort algorithm?
    b)* Use the bubble sort algorithm to sort these fruit into alphabetical order:
        Orange, Banana, Apple, Peach, Grape, Lime ☑
14) What are the four steps of the merge sort algorithm? ☑
15)*Here is a list of numbers:

   8, 7, 5, 1, 3, 6, 4, 2

   a) Use the merge sort algorithm to sort this list into ascending order.
   b) Use the bubble sort algorithm to sort this list into descending order. ☑
16) Outline the strengths and weaknesses of the following sorting algorithms:
    a) bubble sort   b) merge sort ☑
17) Perform a beauty sort on my pets. ☑

Programming Basics — Data Types

Ah my favourite section of the book — it's time to get to grips with some programming...

Everything we cover on pages 8-22 will work slightly differently in different programming languages, but the principles are the same. Pages 23-27 will explain how to use these principles in Python®.

In this section, examples of code will be given in these boxes and will be written in pseudo-code (p2).

The output of the code will be shown in this box.

Programming languages have Five Main Data Types

1) Programming languages store data as different <u>types</u>. You need to learn the ones in this table...

Data type	Pseudo-code	Characteristics	Examples
Integer	INT	Whole numbers only.	0, 6, 10293, –999
Real (or float)	REAL	Numbers that have a decimal part.	0.15, –5.87, 100.0
Boolean	BOOL	Can only take one of two values, usually TRUE or FALSE.	True/False, 1/0, yes/no
Character	CHAR	A single letter, number, symbol.	'A', 'k', '5', '–', '$'
String	STRING	Used to represent text, it is a collection of characters.	'FsTmQ2', '$money$'

2) Each data type is allocated a different amount of <u>memory</u>.

3) Using the correct data types makes code more <u>memory efficient</u>, <u>robust</u> (hard to break) and <u>predictable</u>.

Data type	Typical amount of memory taken up
Integer	2 bytes or 4 bytes.
Real	4 bytes or 8 bytes.
Boolean	1 bit is needed but 1 byte is usually used.
Character	1 byte
String	1 byte for every character in the string.

Programming languages can be <u>weakly typed</u> or <u>strongly typed</u>. Weakly typed languages will try to <u>convert</u> data types to <u>avoid errors</u>, however this can lead to <u>unpredictable results</u>. Strongly typed languages won't try to convert data types and so will produce <u>more errors</u> but more <u>predictable results</u>.

You can Change from one Data Type to another

1) Languages have <u>functions</u> (p21) that let you manually convert between data types — this is known as <u>casting</u>. Different languages will do this in <u>different ways</u> but the principle is the same:

`STRING_TO_INT('1')` — Converts the <u>string '1'</u> to the <u>integer 1</u>.

`STRING_TO_REAL('1.0')` — Converts the <u>string '1.0'</u> to the <u>real 1.0</u>

`INT_TO_STRING(1)` — Converts the <u>integer 1</u> to the <u>string '1'</u>.

`REAL_TO_STRING(1.0)` — Converts the <u>real 1.0</u> to the <u>string '1.0'</u>

2) It's important to realise that the <u>integer 1</u>, the <u>real 1.0</u> and the <u>strings '1'</u> and <u>'1.0'</u> are all different.

3) You can also find the <u>ASCII code</u> (see p43) of <u>characters</u> and vice versa using these functions.

`CHAR_TO_CODE('b')` — Converts the <u>character 'b'</u> into its <u>ASCII code 98</u>.

`CODE_TO_CHAR(98)` — Converts the <u>ASCII code 98</u> into its equivalent <u>character 'b'</u>.

Using the Correct Data Type for different Variables

You should be able to choose the best data type to use in different situations.

EXAMPLE: Give the appropriate data type for each of the categories in this registration form.

Initial of first name:	N
Surname:	Chapman
Age (in whole years):	27
Height (in metres):	1.64
Student:	Yes

Initial of first name should be stored as a character.

Surname should be stored as a string.

Age (in whole years) should be stored as an integer.

Height (in metres) should be stored as a real data type.

Whether or not they are a student could be stored as Boolean.

Will you data? Nah, she's not really my type...

Using the correct data types is a fundamental part of programming — sometimes a piece of data could take different data types and you'll have to decide which is best based on the context of the question.

Programming Basics — Operators

Operators are <u>special characters</u> that perform certain functions. You'll already be used to using operators in maths, but it's important to know how they work in computer science too.

The Basic Arithmetic Operators are straightforward

1) The arithmetic operators take <u>two values</u> and perform a maths <u>function</u> on them.

2) <u>Addition</u>, <u>subtraction</u>, <u>multiplication</u> and <u>division</u> operators do what you'd expect.

3) The <u>DIV operator</u> returns the <u>whole number part</u> of a division and the <u>MOD operator</u> gives the <u>remainder</u>.

Dividing integers might behave oddly in some programming languages, e.g. 5 / 2 may give the answer 2 instead of 2.5...

...using DIV and MOD can avoid these issues.

Function	Typical Operator	Example	Result
Addition	+	5 + 5	10
Subtraction	–	3 – 10	–7
Multiplication	*	4 * 8	32
Division	/	7.5 / 5	1.5
Integer division (quotient)	DIV	20 DIV 3	6
Remainder (modulus)	MOD or %	20 MOD 3	2

4) The first four operators in the table above work on <u>integers</u> and <u>real</u> data values (or combinations of the two). DIV and MOD are for <u>integers only</u>.

5) Computers follow the rule of <u>BODMAS</u> (Brackets, Other, Division, Multiplication, Addition & Subtraction) — so <u>take care</u> when using operators to make sure your code is actually doing what you want it to. E.g. 2 + 8 * 2 will give 18. To do the addition first, use brackets: (2 + 8) * 2 will give 20.

Assignment and Comparison Operators

The <u>assignment operator</u>, ← (or =), is used to <u>assign values</u> to <u>constants</u> or <u>variables</u> (see next pg).

The name of the constant or variable should be on the <u>left hand side</u> of the ←.

```
total ← 25
cost ← total * 3
n ← n + 5
```

Whatever you're assigning to it should be on the <u>right hand side</u>.

This increases the value of n by 5.

<u>Comparison operators</u> compare the expression on their <u>left hand side</u> to the expression on their <u>right hand side</u> and produce a <u>Boolean value</u> (either true or false).

Comparison operator	What it means	Evaluates to True	Evaluates to False
= (or ==)	Is equal to	5 = 5	5 = 8
≠ (or <> or !=)	Is not equal to	6 ≠ 7	6 ≠ 6
<	Is less than	4 < 10	3 < 2
>	Is greater than	15 > 9	10 > 12
≤ (or <=)	Is less than or equal to	7 ≤ 8	11 ≤ 10
≥ (or >=)	Is greater than or equal to	3 ≥ 3	9 ≥ 12

1) Many programming languages use "=" for the <u>assignment operator</u> and "==" for the <u>comparison operator</u>. A common mistake is to get them the wrong way round — you'll know if you've used them <u>incorrectly</u> because your code won't do what you were expecting.

2) In this book, pseudo-code will always be written using <u>← for assignment</u> and <u>= for "is equal to"</u> so that it is clear when values are being assigned, and when we are doing a comparison.

All these operators and not a surgeon in sight, PANIC...

Operators are fundamental to programming, so make sure you get to grips with them now.
they'll use the operators on this page but the programming language you study might be a

Constants and Variables

Now that you know about the different data types and operations it's time to look at constants and variables. As you can probably tell by the names, constants remain the same and variables can be changed.

Data Values can be Constants or Variables

1) Data values can be stored as constants or variables.

2) The name of the constant or variable is linked to a memory location that stores the data value. The size of the memory location depends on the data type (see p8).

3) A constant is assigned a value at design time that can't be changed. If you attempt to change the value of a constant in a program then the interpreter or compiler (see p60) will return an error.

4) Variables on the other hand can change value which makes them far more useful than constants.

5) In many programming languages, constants and variables need to be declared before you can use them. When writing pseudo-code they're often just declared when you want to assign a value to them. This can be done in different ways:

Here are two ways of declaring PRESSURE as a constant and assigning it the value of 30. Upper case letters are often used when naming constants.

The second example in each case specifies the data type as well. A colon, ':', is used to separate the name of the variable and the data type.

Here are two ways of declaring temperature as a variable and assigning it the value of 20.5.

```
CONSTANT PRESSURE ← 30
CONSTANT PRESSURE: Integer ← 30
```

```
temperature ← 20.5
temperature: Real ← 20.5
```

To make code easier to follow, programmers usually give variables and constants descriptive names. They will also follow standard naming conventions when naming variables. For example, by capitalising the first letter of each word (apart from the first), like tempInOven or pressureInPot.

Identifying Constants and Variables in Programs

EXAMPLE:

In a multi-event athletics competition, athletes get 5 points for winning an event and 2 points for coming second. Otherwise they get 0 points. This program calculates the total number of points that an athlete has.

```
firsts ← USERINPUT
seconds ← USERINPUT
OUTPUT (5 * firsts + 2 * seconds)
```

a) Rewrite the program so that all the variables are declared with data types and initial values.

The two variables are firsts and seconds. They should both be declared as integers as there are a whole number of events.

```
firsts: Integer ← 0
seconds: Integer ← 0
firsts ← USERINPUT
seconds ← USERINPUT
OUTPUT (5 * firsts + 2 * seconds)
```

The initial value of each variable is set to 0.

b) Give two reasons for assigning the values 5 and 2 to constants.

- They don't need to be changed during the running of the program.
- If the points awarded for each event was changed you'd only need to change the value given in the declaration of the constant.

This is an example of improving the maintainability (p29) of the program.

A constant, a variable... and finally a constant. Time starts now...

In some programming languages, you can't change the data type of a variable, only the value. But as you saw on p8, you can use a casting function to return a different data type, which you can then assign to a new variable:

```
cost ← 50
stringCost ← INT_TO_STRING(cost)
```

This converts the integer 50 to the string '50' and stores it in stringCost.

Strings

Remember from page 8 that strings are a data type made up of characters — these characters are <u>alphanumeric</u> (letters, numbers, spaces, symbols, etc.). Now you'll see how you can manipulate them.

Strings are written inside *Quotation Marks*

In AQA pseudo-code, strings will be written inside <u>single quotation marks</u> ', but in some programming languages you might see <u>double quotation marks</u> being used ".

```
string1 ← 'Output me, I am a string.'
OUTPUT string1
```
```
Output me, I am a string.
```

Strings can be <u>joined together</u> to form new strings — this is called <u>concatenation</u>. It's often done using the <u>+ operator</u>.

```
string1 ← 'My favourite colour is'
string2 ← 'purple.'
newString ← string1 + ' ' + string2
OUTPUT newString
```
```
My favourite colour is purple.
```

The + operator joins the strings together.

A space character has been added between the two strings.

Programs *let you* Manipulate Strings *in a variety of ways*

1) Before getting started on string manipulation you should know that the <u>characters</u> in a string are usually numbered <u>starting at 0</u>.

```
0 1 2 3 4 5
S P Y I N G
```

2) Here are some common <u>string manipulation</u> functions that you'll need to learn for your exam.

Pseudo-code function	Operation	Example
LEN(string)	Returns the number of characters in the string.	LEN('Hello') returns 5
POSITION(string, character)	Returns the position of the first occurrence of a certain character in the given string.	POSITION('Hello', 'o') returns 4 POSITION('Hello', 'l') returns 2
SUBSTRING(x, y, string)	Extracts a substring from the original string starting at position x and finishing at position y.	SUBSTRING(0, 3, 'Hello') returns 'Hell'

EXAMPLE: An electricity company generates a customer's 7 character username from:
- the first 3 letters of their town.
- the customer's age when they sign up (2 digits).
- the last letter of the customer's surname.

Write an algorithm to generate a username for any customer given that their data is stored under the variables town, age and surname.

Start by working out how to <u>extract</u> the information from <u>each variable</u>...

1) `SUBSTRING(0, 2, town)` ⟵ This extracts the <u>first 3 characters</u> from the customer's town.

2) `INT_TO_STRING(age)` ⟵ <u>Converts</u> the customer's age to a <u>string</u> (p8).

3) `n ← LEN(surname)`
`SUBSTRING(n-1, n-1, surname)` ⟵ Finds the <u>length</u> of the <u>surname</u> so that it can take the <u>last character</u>. Remember, the last character is in the n–1th position.

... then combine the code into a <u>single algorithm</u> at the end.

```
n ← LEN(surname)
username ← SUBSTRING(0, 2, town) + INT_TO_STRING(age) + SUBSTRING(n-1, n-1, surname)
```

I hope you don't just think I'm stringing you along...

Any text that is input or output from a program will be a string, so it's important that you can manipulate them like you've got them wrapped around your little finger. As well as the functions above, the examiners might throw a more obscure one at you in the exam. Luckily they'll also show you exactly how it works.

Program Flow — Selection

The flow of a program is the order that the steps are carried out in. One way that you can control the program flow is by using <u>selection statements</u> — but first, here's how to get your programs to interact with the user.

Programs need to be able to Interact with a User

1) It's really handy for programs to be able to get information from and give information to the <u>user</u> — this is done through the <u>input</u> and <u>output</u> devices.

2) <u>Inputs</u> can be received from many devices, e.g. keyboard, mouse, webcam or microphone.

3) <u>Outputs</u> are typically displayed visually on the monitor or as sound from the speakers.

4) When writing pseudo-code we usually assume that <u>inputs</u> are from a <u>keyboard</u> and <u>outputs</u> will be <u>displayed</u> on a monitor (typically as <u>text</u>).

When you ask a user for an <u>input</u>, you should assign it to a <u>variable</u> with a <u>descriptive name</u>.

```
OUTPUT 'Enter your age'
userAge ← USERINPUT
OUTPUT userAge
```

<u>Outputs</u> can be used to <u>communicate</u> with the user and <u>prompt</u> them to <u>input</u> data.

Outputs will usually be <u>strings</u> — to output data stored in a variable just use the <u>variable name</u>.

IF statements usually have an IF-THEN-ELSE structure

1) <u>IF statements</u> allow you to check if a <u>condition</u> is true or false, and carry out different actions depending on the outcome. You can think about them as a <u>flowchart</u>.

2) Here is a program that can verify if the user knows a certain passcode before granting access.

The first part of the IF statement is the condition that must be checked.

Indenting the actions for each condition makes the code more readable.

```
passcode ← USERINPUT
IF passcode = 'GO' THEN
    OUTPUT 'Unrestricted access.'
ELSE
    OUTPUT 'Access denied.'
ENDIF
```

The part after THEN tells the program what to do if the condition is true.

The part after ELSE tells the program what to do if the condition is false.

3) If there is <u>nothing</u> for the program to do when the <u>condition is false</u>, <u>leave out</u> the '<u>else</u>' part.

Nested IF statements allow multiple outputs

1) More complex IF statements can be made by putting one IF statement <u>inside</u> another one — this type of selection statement is called a <u>nested IF statement</u>.

2) Nested IF statements allow you to <u>check more conditions</u> once you've established that the <u>previous condition</u> is <u>true</u> or <u>false</u>.

If the <u>first condition</u> is <u>true</u>, it will check the <u>second condition</u>...

If the <u>first condition</u> is <u>false</u>, it will run this <u>else statement</u> — all access is denied.

<u>Indentation</u> lets the reader see where each IF statement begins and ends.

```
userType ← USERINPUT
passcode ← USERINPUT
IF passcode = 'GO' THEN
    IF userType = 'Teacher' THEN
        OUTPUT 'Unrestricted access.'
    ELSE
        OUTPUT 'Restricted access.'
    ENDIF
ELSE
    OUTPUT 'Access denied.'
ENDIF
```

If the <u>second condition</u> is <u>true</u> then unrestricted access is allowed.

If the <u>second condition</u> is <u>false</u> then restricted access is allowed.

IF you understand IF statements THEN make yourself a brew...

IF statements are used all the time when writing code — they really are a programmer's best friend. Whenever there is a decision to be made, a friendly IF statement will always be there to help you out.

Program Flow — Selection

A couple more selection statements coming right up, starting with an ELSE-IF statement. Careful with these ones — they might look similar to nested IF statements, but they are different. Have a look below...

ELSE-IF statements *check conditions until one is True*

1) ELSE-IF statements are used to check multiple conditions and give different outputs depending on which condition is true.

2) They are different from nested IF statements as they only check more conditions if the previous condition is false — e.g. IF the first condition is true then they won't check the others.

The conditions are all indented to the same level.

```
userType ← USERINPUT
IF userType = 'Teacher' THEN
    OUTPUT 'Unrestricted access.'
ELSE IF userType = 'Parent' THEN
    OUTPUT 'Level 1 restricted access.'
ELSE IF userType = 'Pupil' THEN
    OUTPUT 'Level 2 restricted access.'
ELSE
    OUTPUT 'Access denied.'
ENDIF
```

If all conditions are false then the program will deny all access.

The first condition is always checked — if it's true then it will allow unrestricted access.

The second condition is checked if the first condition is false — if it's true then it will allow level 1 restricted access.

The third condition is checked if the first and second conditions are false — if it's true then it will allow level 2 restricted access.

CASE Statements *check the value of a Variable*

1) Instead of checking to see if a condition is true or false, CASE statements (sometimes called SWITCH statements) can check if a variable has specific values.

2) They're used when you want a program to perform different actions for different values of the same variable.

3) Here is a program that can be used to count votes in an election.

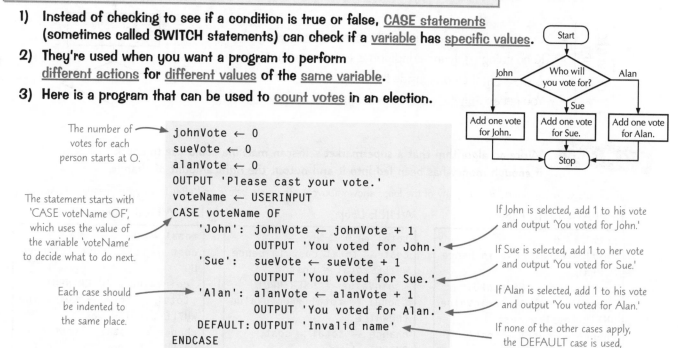

The number of votes for each person starts at 0.

```
johnVote ← 0
sueVote ← 0
alanVote ← 0
OUTPUT 'Please cast your vote.'
voteName ← USERINPUT
CASE voteName OF
    'John': johnVote ← johnVote + 1
            OUTPUT 'You voted for John.'
    'Sue':  sueVote ← sueVote + 1
            OUTPUT 'You voted for Sue.'
    'Alan': alanVote ← alanVote + 1
            OUTPUT 'You voted for Alan.'
    DEFAULT: OUTPUT 'Invalid name'
ENDCASE
```

The statement starts with 'CASE voteName OF', which uses the value of the variable 'voteName' to decide what to do next.

Each case should be indented to the same place.

If John is selected, add 1 to his vote and output 'You voted for John.'

If Sue is selected, add 1 to her vote and output 'You voted for Sue.'

If Alan is selected, add 1 to his vote and output 'You voted for Alan.'

If none of the other cases apply, the DEFAULT case is used, and 'Invalid name' is output.

4) CASE statements have a similar structure to ELSE-IF statements but they give a neater way to test different values of a variable — this makes them easier than ELSE-IF statements to maintain.

5) The drawback of CASE statements is that they can only check the value of one variable. ELSE-IF statements can check if multiple conditions are true.

> ELSE-IF and CASE statements can also be used to make more complex nested selection statements just like the nested IF statements on p12.

Can't decide what to have for lunch? Use a selection statement...

It's a good idea to include a "default" case with CASE statements — it tells the program what to do if none of the other cases are correct. This is useful as it can help make CASE statements more robust.

Program Flow — Iteration

Now it's time to have a look at some <u>iteration statements</u>. The statements on this page are all <u>indefinite</u> iteration statements — so the number of times that they repeat depends on a <u>condition</u>.

All these Loops are controlled by Conditions

<u>REPEAT-UNTIL</u>, <u>WHILE</u> and <u>DO-WHILE</u> loops are easy to get mixed up — they're very similar but with subtle differences that you need to know:

> You might also see a DO-UNTIL loop — this does the same thing as a REPEAT-UNTIL loop.

REPEAT-UNTIL LOOPS
- Controlled by a condition at the <u>end of the loop</u>.
- Keep going <u>until</u> the condition is <u>true</u> (i.e. while it is false).
- <u>Always run</u> the code inside them <u>at least once</u>.
- You get an <u>infinite loop</u> if the condition is <u>never true</u>.

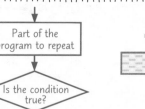

WHILE LOOPS
- Controlled by a condition at the <u>start of the loop</u>.
- Keep going <u>while</u> the condition is <u>true</u> (i.e. until it is false).
- <u>Never run</u> the code inside them if the condition is initially <u>false</u>.
- You get an <u>infinite loop</u> if the condition is <u>always true</u>.

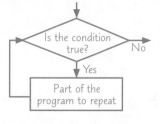

DO-WHILE LOOPS
- Controlled by a condition at the <u>end of the loop</u>.
- Keep going <u>while</u> the condition is <u>true</u> (i.e. until it is false).
- <u>Always run</u> the code inside them <u>at least once</u>.
- You get an <u>infinite loop</u> if the condition is <u>always true</u>.

EXAMPLE: Write an algorithm that a supermarket self-scan machine could use to check if enough money has been fed into it and output the right amount of change.

You could write an algorithm using any of the loops shown above — the code before and after the loop is exactly the same.

REPEAT-UNTIL Loop:
```
total ← 0
cost ← total cost in pence
REPEAT
 coinValue ← USERINPUT
 total ← total + coinValue
UNTIL total ≥ cost
change ← total - cost
OUTPUT change
```
The loop starts at <u>REPEAT</u> and ends when the <u>UNTIL</u> condition is <u>true</u> — when the total is greater than or equal to the cost.

WHILE Loop:
```
total ← 0
cost ← total cost in pence
WHILE total < cost
 coinValue ← USERINPUT
 total ← total + coinValue
ENDWHILE
change ← total - cost
OUTPUT change
```
The loop starts by checking the <u>WHILE</u> condition is <u>true</u> and keeps repeating until it is <u>false</u> — when the total is greater than or equal to the cost.

DO-WHILE Loop:
```
total ← 0
cost ← total cost in pence
DO
 coinValue ← USERINPUT
 total ← total + coinValue
WHILE total < cost
change ← total - cost
OUTPUT change
```
The loop starts at <u>DO</u> and repeats until the <u>WHILE</u> condition is <u>false</u> — when the total is greater than or equal to the cost.

> All of these loops work exactly the same when cost > 0. If the cost is 0, the WHILE loop won't expect an input, whereas the REPEAT-UNTIL and DO-WHILE loops will.

All these loops and not a roller coaster in sight, what a shame...

It's important that you learn the similarities and differences between all of these condition-controlled loops so that they don't all merge into one. The key thing is recognising exactly when the loop will stop.

Program Flow — Iteration

The final type of iteration statement you need to know about is the FOR loop — it's a type of <u>definite</u> iteration so it will repeat for the exact number of times you tell it to. What a well-behaved little iteration statement.

FOR Loops are an example of a Count-Controlled Loop

1) <u>FOR loops</u> will repeat the code inside them a fixed number of times. The number of times that the code repeats will depend on an <u>initial value</u>, <u>end value</u> and sometimes a <u>step count</u>.

2) For example, FOR k ← 1 TO 10 STEP 3 will count up from 1 to 10 in steps of 3, so k ← 1, k ← 4, k ← 7 and k ← 10. If no step count is given the count will <u>increase by 1</u> each time.

The FOR loop repeats the code between FOR and ENDFOR.

3) The <u>number of times</u> the loop repeats can also be set as the <u>program runs</u> — e.g. FOR k ← 1 TO x, where x is a variable.

4) FOR loops can also use the count <u>within the loop</u> — in the example on the right, k is used to keep track of how many votes have been cast.

Loops can contain other types of statement — the CASE statement used here is from p13.

```
johnVote ← 0
sueVote ← 0
alanVote ← 0
FOR k ← 1 TO 100          Allows 100 votes to be cast.
  OUTPUT 'Please cast your vote.'
  voteName ← USERINPUT
  CASE voteName OF
    'John': johnVote ← johnVote + 1
            OUTPUT 'You voted for John.'
    'Sue':  sueVote ← sueVote + 1
            OUTPUT 'You've voted for Sue.'
    'Alan': alanVote ← alanVote + 1
            OUTPUT 'You voted for Alan.'
    DEFAULT:OUTPUT 'Invalid name'
  ENDCASE
  OUTPUT INT_TO_STRING(k) + ' total votes'
ENDFOR
```

The value of k can be used anywhere within the loop.

```
cheerName ← 'CGP'
FOR letter IN cheerName
    OUTPUT ('Give me a ' + letter + '!')
ENDFOR
```

```
Give me a C!
Give me a G!
Give me a P!
```

5) You can also loop through all the <u>characters</u> in a <u>string</u> using a <u>FOR-IN statement</u>.

6) This can be really useful for things like <u>input validation</u> — see page 30.

Nested Iteration statements have Loops Within loops

1) Nested iteration statements will typically just have <u>one loop</u> inside <u>another loop</u> (an <u>outer</u> loop and an <u>inner</u> loop). But they can get quite complicated when you start <u>adding more loops</u> — you get loops within loops within loops... etc.

2) <u>Every time</u> the outer loop repeats, the inner loop completes a <u>full set</u> of iterations.

Nested iteration is really useful when you're working with two-dimensional arrays — see p19.

3) This example shows a <u>FOR loop</u> inside a <u>REPEAT-UNTIL loop</u>. The algorithm is for a darts practice machine, where the player tries to get a score of <u>100 or more</u> in <u>3 darts</u>, and the machine counts <u>how many attempts</u> it takes them to do it.

At the start of each iteration of the REPEAT loop, the number of attempts taken increases by 1 and the current total is reset to 0.

The REPEAT loop ends when the player scores 100 points or more in one round.

```
attempt ← 0
REPEAT
    attempt ← attempt + 1
    total ← 0
    FOR dart ← 1 TO 3
      OUTPUT 'Enter score for throw'
      score ← USERINPUT
      total ← total + score
    ENDFOR
UNTIL total ≥ 100
OUTPUT INT_TO_STRING(attempt) + ' attempts taken.'
```

Each time you go through the REPEAT loop, the FOR loop repeats 3 times.

On every iteration of the FOR loop, the player enters their score and it is added to their total for that attempt.

FOR k ← 0 TO 1 000 000, send us a batch of muffins, ENDFOR...

When you're putting nested iteration statements into your own programs, you can use any combination of definite and indefinite loops. Just be careful that you don't get stuck looping around forever and ever.

Boolean Operators

Boolean operators work with Boolean values to produce a Boolean answer — that's a whole lot of Booleans in one sentence. Learn the stuff on this page and one day you'll be a Booleanaire, just like me.

AND, OR and NOT are the only Boolean Operators you'll need

1) It doesn't make sense to use the arithmetic operators on things that are either <u>true or false</u> so instead you use the Boolean operators <u>AND</u>, <u>OR</u> and <u>NOT</u>.

Boolean operator	Examples that return true	Examples that return false
AND	$3 < 5$ AND $2 > 1$	$4 \leq 5$ AND $10 > 20$
OR	$1 > 8$ OR $2 = 2$	$1 = 8$ OR $2 < 2$
NOT	NOT($5 > 8$)	NOT($10 > 6$)

In some code you might see AND written as &&, OR written as || and NOT written as !

2) Just like with numerical operators, you can <u>combine Boolean operators</u> — it's important that you use <u>brackets</u> in long Boolean expressions to let the computer know which part to do <u>first</u>. <u>Boolean operations</u> are carried out in the following <u>order</u>: brackets, NOT, AND then OR.

Boolean Operators can be used in Conditions

Boolean operators can be used in selection and iteration statements (p12-15) to check <u>multiple conditions</u>.

1. Karen and Stu are playing a 'best out of 10' game. The game should end when one of them wins 6 rounds or they both win 5 rounds. Write an algorithm to keep score in the game.

```
karenRounds ← 0
stuRounds ← 0
REPEAT
    OUTPUT 'Enter the name of the round winner'
    roundWinner ← USERINPUT                    There's a CASE statement within the loop. This is
    CASE roundWinner OF  ◄————————— where good indentation in your pseudo-code is key.
        'Karen': karenRounds ← karenRounds + 1
        'Stu': stuRounds ← stuRounds + 1        The REPEAT-UNTIL loop stops when
    ENDCASE                                     one of these three conditions is met.
UNTIL karenRounds = 6 OR stuRounds = 6 OR (karenRounds = 5 AND stuRounds = 5)
```

2. In a computer game a character's status depends on three variables: hunger, hydration and comfort. If any of the conditions on the right are met then the character dies, otherwise they are alive.

- Any of the variables are equal to 0.
- Any two of the variables are less than 20.
- All three of the variables are less than 40.

Write an algorithm to work out the status of the character.

```
IF hunger = 0 OR hydration = 0 OR comfort = 0 THEN
    alive ← false
ELSE IF (hunger < 20 AND hydration < 20) OR (hunger < 20 AND comfort < 20)
        OR (hydration < 20 AND comfort < 20) THEN
    alive ← false
ELSE IF hunger < 40 AND hydration < 40 AND comfort < 40 THEN
    alive ← false
ELSE
    alive ← true
ENDIF
```

Anyone caught Boolean other pupils will be given detention...

Make sure you can use Boolean operators in your programs — they can save lots of work by letting you check lots of conditions at the same time. There is more about how Boolean operators work on p34-35.

Random Number Generation

Random numbers are really useful when you don't want your programs to do the same thing every time. They can be used to simulate random real-life events, e.g. rolling a dice, picking raffle tickets, etc.

Random Numbers are useful when making *Games*

1) Random numbers can be used in <u>simple games</u> when the programmer wants a number to be <u>unknown</u> — even the programmer themselves won't know what it's going to be.

2) Most programming languages have functions to <u>generate random numbers</u> — in pseudo-code, <u>random integers</u> can be generated using this function:

```
RANDOM_INT(x, y)
```
Generates a random integer between x and y (including x and y).

3) Here is an example of how random numbers can be used to simulate a roll of a <u>6-sided dice</u>.

Will randomly generate either 1, 2, 3, 4, 5 or 6 and assign it to the variable 'roll'.

Here, the number it has randomly generated is 2.

```
roll ← RANDOM_INT(1, 6)
OUTPUT roll
```
```
2
```

4) <u>FOR loops</u> can be used when you want to generate a <u>whole bunch</u> of random numbers.

This FOR loop will generate five random numbers from 1 to 10.

```
FOR i ← 1 TO 5
    roll ← RANDOM_INT(1, 10)
    OUTPUT roll
ENDFOR
```

The output will look something like...

```
4
9
4
2
10
```

Note that the same number can be randomly generated more than once.

You can use Random Numbers to make Random Selections

1) Instead of outputting the random number that you generated, you can use it to randomly generate <u>another event</u>.

2) Suppose you want to <u>simulate a coin toss</u> — there are two outcomes, <u>heads</u> or <u>tails</u> — we can simplify this in programming terms to 0 and 1 (where 0 = heads, 1 = tails).

Heads I win, tails you lose...

```
number ← RANDOM_INT(0, 1)
IF number = 0 THEN
    OUTPUT 'Heads'
ELSE IF number = 1 THEN
    OUTPUT 'Tails'
ENDIF
```

Randomly generates either 0 or 1.

Technically, you could have an ELSE statement at the bottom without the condition, because there are only two possible outcomes.

3) Random numbers are really handy to use with <u>arrays</u> (see p18-19). You can generate a <u>random number</u> then pick the element in that <u>position</u> of the array.

Uses the random number to select a piece of fruit from the array.

The random number generated was 3, so the fruit that was chosen was 'Peach' — as numbering in an array starts at 0.

```
fruits ← ['Mango', 'Banana', 'Pear', 'Peach']
number ← RANDOM_INT(0, 3)
chosenFruit ← fruits[number]
OUTPUT number
OUTPUT 'Today you should eat a ' + chosenFruit
```
```
3
Today you should eat a Peach
```

Randomly generates either 0, 1, 2 or 3.

1, 1, 1, 1, 1, 1, 1 — I think my random number generator is broken...

The random numbers that are generated in a programming language are called pseudo-random numbers because they aren't completely random, they just look like they are. They are usually generated by following a complex algorithm which means that they will have a pattern — it's just very hard to see it...

Arrays

When you need to store data within a program you can do it using variables. But if you have lots of similar data to store, then using variables for each one is inefficient and that's where arrays come in. Hip, hip, array!

Arrays *are used to store multiple Data Values*

1) An array is a <u>data structure</u> that can store a group of data values, of the <u>same type</u>, under <u>one name</u>.

2) Each piece of data in an array is called an <u>element</u> — each element can be <u>accessed</u> using its <u>position</u> (or <u>index</u>) in the array.

A data structure is a format for storing data — other data structures include records and files.

3) Arrays are <u>most helpful</u> when you have lots of <u>related data</u> that you want to store and it doesn't make sense to use <u>separate variables</u> — e.g. the names of pupils in a class, marks in a test, etc.

4) Just like variables, some languages require you to <u>declare arrays</u> before you use them.

One-Dimensional Arrays *are like Lists*

The easiest way to get your head around <u>one-dimensional arrays</u> is to picture them as <u>lists</u>. Different languages have lots of fancy ways to <u>create</u> and <u>update arrays</u>. Here are the ones you'll need to learn for your exam:

1) Creating arrays — just like variables, you start off with the <u>array name</u> and the <u>assignment operator</u>. Then put your data values inside <u>square brackets [ ]</u> with <u>commas</u> separating each value.

```
rowers ← ['Jada', 'Adam', 'Shelly', 'Amira']
```
Here the strings '<u>Jada</u>', '<u>Adam</u>', '<u>Shelly</u>' and '<u>Amira</u>' are in positions <u>0</u>, <u>1</u>, <u>2</u> and <u>3</u> of the <u>rowers</u> array.

2) Retrieving elements from an array can be done by using the <u>name</u> of the array and the <u>element's position</u>. Remember that positions are numbered <u>starting at 0</u>.

```
OUTPUT rowers[0]
```
```
Jada
```

3) Changing elements is done by reassigning the array position to a different data value.

Replaces the rower in position 0 with 'Tamal'.
```
rowers[0] ← 'Tamal'
OUTPUT rowers
```
```
['Tamal', 'Adam', 'Shelly', 'Amira']
```
Notice that 'Jada' has been completely removed from the array.

4) The <u>number of elements</u> in an array can be found using the <u>LEN()</u> function — just like for strings (see p11).
```
LEN(rowers)
```
```
4
```

Combining these <u>array functions</u> with <u>FOR loops</u> (see p15) will give you a <u>systematic way</u> of accessing and changing all of the <u>elements</u> in an array. Amongst other things, FOR loops can be used to <u>search</u> for specific elements, or make a similar change to <u>lots of elements</u>.

EXAMPLE: The numbers below are stored in an array called scores. Write an algorithm that will add 3 to each element of the scores array.

4	12	32	18	21	11	9	14	24

FOR loop will run on each element of the array — e.g. from position 0 to position 8
```
FOR k ← 0 TO LEN(scores)-1
    scores[k] ← scores[k] + 3
ENDFOR
```
Adds 3 to the element in position k of the array.

Oh, you were expecting me to make some sort of arraysing pun...

For the exam, remember that arrays can only store one data type and that you can't change the size of them once they've been declared. However, some programming languages (e.g. PHP) have arrays that are much more flexible data structures — they can store different data types and their size can be altered.

Arrays

Now that you've covered one-dimensional arrays, the only way is up — that's right, two-dimensional arrays. Arrays can have even more dimensions, but luckily the examiners have decided that two is enough.

Two-Dimensional Arrays are like a List Of Lists

You can think of two-dimensional arrays as one-dimensional arrays where each element is also a one-dimensional array.

You can visualise arrays as tables or grids.

	0	1
0	oak	ash
1	beech	cedar
2	pine	elm

```
trees ← [['oak', 'ash'], ['beech', 'cedar'], ['pine', 'elm']]
```

The position of an element is usually written as [a][b] or [a, b], where a represents the position of the one-dimensional list that the element is in and b represents its position within that one-dimensional list.

```
OUTPUT 'My favourite tree is ' + trees[0][0]
OUTPUT 'My 2nd favourite tree is ' + trees[2][1]
```

```
My favourite tree is oak
My 2nd favourite tree is elm
```

You can change elements in exactly the same way as you saw for one-dimensional arrays (p18).

You can also use the LEN() function on an array or on an element in the array.

```
LEN(trees)
```
```
3
```

```
LEN(trees[1])
```
```
2
```

Two-Dimensional Array Example

EXAMPLE: The 'scores' array has been used to store four test scores for five pupils, as shown. E.g. scores[2][0] will return the test 2 score for pupil 0, which is 5.

		Pupils				
		0	1	2	3	4
Tests	0	15	5	13	12	7
	1	2	14	11	14	9
	2	5	4	12	7	13
	3	6	8	18	19	15

a) Evaluate scores[3][2] / scores[1][0].

scores[3][2] = 18 and scores[1][0] = 2

So scores[3][2] / scores[1][0] = 18/2 = 9

b) Write an algorithm to count the total score of any given pupil.

As there aren't very many scores you could just add them together. E.g. for pupil 0 you could do scores[0][0] + scores[1][0] + scores[2][0] + scores[3][0]. But it's better practice to use a loop as it is easier to edit.

```
total ← 0
OUTPUT 'Enter the number of the pupil'
pupil ← USERINPUT
FOR i ← 0 TO 3
    total ← total + scores[i][pupil]
ENDFOR
OUTPUT total
```

c) The pass mark on every test was 9 or above. Write an algorithm to count the number of passes in the original array.

The passTotal variable keeps track of how many values are passes.

The i FOR loop searches each row and the j FOR loop searches each column.

The IF statement checks if the value in position [i][j] is a pass and adds 1 to passTotal if it is.

Finally passTotal is output.

```
passTotal ← 0
FOR i ← 0 TO 3
    FOR j ← 0 TO 4
        IF scores[i][j] ≥ 9 THEN
            passTotal ← passTotal + 1
        ENDIF
    ENDFOR
ENDFOR
OUTPUT INT_TO_STRING(passTotal) + ' passes.'
```

This is an example of a nested FOR loop.

After that last pun, I'd say that I definitely deserve arrays...

Two-dimensional arrays can be used to store information about a digital image — each pixel's information can be stored as an element in the array. Programmers can then manipulate the image using array commands, e.g. changing the values of pixels, cutting rows and columns out of the image, etc.

Records

Records aren't just those big black round things that look like burnt CDs, they're also a useful data structure...

Records can contain Different Data Types

1) A record is a type of data structure (like an array — see p18), which means that it is used to store a collection of data values.

> In the context of a database table (see p61), a record is just a row of data.

2) One of the things that makes records so useful is that, unlike arrays, they can store values with different data types (see p8), such as strings, integers and Booleans.

3) Each item in a record is called a field (or attribute), and each field is given a data type and a field name when the record is created. The field name can help to describe the data stored in that field of the record.

> Different programming languages have slight variations on record data structures. E.g. Python® has dictionaries, and C# has structures.

4) Records are fixed in length, which means that you can't add extra fields to them once they've been created.

Records can keep Related Information in one place

1) When you create a record structure, you can assign a name and a data type to each field:

```
RECORD recipe1
    recipeNumber : Integer
    recipeName : String
    tested : Boolean
    score : Integer
ENDRECORD
```

The record is called 'recipe1'.

Each field has its own data type.

'recipeNumber', 'recipeName', 'tested' and 'score' are the fields of the record.

2) Once you've created the structure of your record, you can assign values to the different fields:

```
recipe1.recipeNumber ← 1
recipe1.recipeName ← 'Chocolate Cake'
recipe1.tested ← False
recipe1.score ← 0
```

The data assigned to each field needs to have the correct data type. E.g. 'tested', should be assigned a Boolean value.

3) You can use the record name to access a whole record. Or you can use the record name with a field name to access a particular item of a record.

```
OUTPUT recipe1
OUTPUT recipe1.recipeName

(1, 'Chocolate Cake', False, 0)
Chocolate Cake
```

Individual items in a record can be accessed and changed.

```
recipe1.tested ← True
recipe1.score ← 6
OUTPUT recipe1.recipeName + ' scored '
       + INT_TO_STRING(recipe1.score)

Chocolate Cake scored 6
```

Arrays are handy if you want to Group Records together

If you have multiple records with the same structure, it can be useful to collect them together in an array.

```
recipeBook ← [recipe1, recipe2, recipe3]
FOR i ← 0 TO 2
    IF recipeBook[i].score ≥ 7 THEN
        OUTPUT recipeBook[i].recipeName
    ENDIF
ENDFOR
Coconut Cookies
```

recipe2 and recipe3 have the same structure as recipe1 but different values.

This will output the names of all recipes with a score ≥ 7.

You can visualise the recipeBook array as a table:

	recipeNumber	recipeName	tested	score
0	1	Chocolate Cake	True	6
1	2	Lemon Slice	True	3
2	3	Coconut Cookies	True	8

Well, we got through all that in record time...

There are some key differences between records in databases and in programming — these records aren't automatically collected in one place, so you need to group them together manually, e.g. using an array.

Subroutines

Subroutines (or sub programs) can be used to save time and to simplify code. By now you'll definitely have come across them even if you don't know what they are yet — all is explained on the next two pages.

Subroutines *help to avoid Repeating Code*

1) <u>Subroutines</u> are <u>sets of instructions</u> stored under <u>one name</u> — when you want your program to do the whole set of instructions you only need to <u>call the name</u> of the subroutine.

2) Subroutines can be either <u>functions</u> or <u>procedures</u> — the main difference is that functions always <u>return a value</u> and procedures do not.

3) Subroutines are very useful when you have sets of instructions that you need to <u>repeat</u> in different places within a program. They give your program more <u>structure</u> and <u>readability</u> whilst cutting down on the <u>amount of code</u> you actually need to write.

4) High-level programming languages (see p60) have <u>common</u> subroutines <u>built into them</u>. If you want one that does something <u>more specific</u> you can <u>create them</u> yourself.

```
# The max() subroutine returns the highest value.
x ← max(12, 21, 8, 9, 19)
```

5) In most subroutines you'll encounter <u>parameters</u>.

<u>Parameters</u> are special variables used to pass values into a subroutine. Each parameter will have a <u>name</u>, and in some languages you can specify a <u>data type</u> and a <u>default value</u>.

The actual values that the parameters take when the subroutine is called are sometimes called <u>arguments</u>.

Subroutines *can carry out a Set Of Instructions*

1) Subroutines don't have to take <u>parameters</u>...   ...but they <u>sometimes will</u>.

'name' is a parameter.

```
SUBROUTINE welcome()
    OUTPUT 'Hello and welcome.'
    OUTPUT 'This is a procedure.'
ENDSUBROUTINE
```

```
SUBROUTINE betterWelcome(name)
    OUTPUT 'Hello ' + name + ' and welcome.'
    OUTPUT 'This is a procedure.'
ENDSUBROUTINE
```

2) Subroutines are called by <u>typing their name</u> (and giving <u>parameters</u> if necessary).

```
welcome()
```
```
Hello and welcome.
This is a procedure.
```

```
betterWelcome('Pablo')
```
```
Hello Pablo and welcome.
This is a procedure.
```

The string 'Pablo' is passed into the betterWelcome subroutine.

3) Note that subroutines that <u>don't</u> return a value are called <u>procedures</u>.

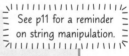

PROCEDURE SHOP

We have a strict <u>no returns</u> policy.

Functions *will always Return a Value*

1) Subroutines that <u>return a value</u> are called <u>functions</u>.

2) When a function is called it should be <u>assigned</u> to a <u>variable</u> or used in a <u>statement</u> otherwise the value that it returns will not be stored anywhere and will be lost.

 EXAMPLE: Write a subroutine to join two strings together with a space between them and show it working on the strings 'computer' and 'science'.

See p11 for a reminder on string manipulation.

Use RETURN to pass a value out of the subroutine.

```
SUBROUTINE joinStrings(string1, string2)
    RETURN string1 + ' ' + string2
ENDSUBROUTINE
subject ← joinStrings('computer', 'science')
OUTPUT subject
```
```
computer science
```

string1 and string2 are parameters.

'computer' and 'science' are passed into the subroutine.

The result is stored as the variable 'subject'.

So is a parameter longer or shorter than a kilometre?

When you're actually programming with subroutines they are written as a separate block of code to the main program. They are then used by the main program when you want to perform a specific operation.

Subroutines

Ah, just what the doctor ordered, another page on subroutines — and this one is even better. Trust me.

Subroutines *can contain anything covered in this Section*

EXAMPLE: Orla has been given a maths problem to add together all of the numbers between two integers (including the integers themselves) and work out if the total is divisible by 7.

Write a subroutine that Orla could use to solve the maths problem for any pair of integers.

The variable 'total' is defined inside the subroutine so it's a local variable (see below).

The IF statement checks if the total is divisible by 7. Remember, MOD will give the remainder of a division (p9).

```
SUBROUTINE addIntegers(x, y)
    total ← 0
    FOR i ← x TO y
        total ← total + i
    ENDFOR
    IF total MOD 7 = 0 THEN
        divisible ← true
    ELSE
        divisible ← false
    ENDIF
    RETURN divisible
ENDSUBROUTINE
```

x and y are the parameters of the subroutine.

The FOR loop is used to add up all the integers from x to y.

The variable 'divisible' is set to True or False depending on the outcome of the IF statement.

The subroutine is a function as it returns a value.

Variables *can be local or global*

1) All variables have a <u>scope</u> (either local or global) — the scope of a variable tells you <u>which parts</u> of the program the variable can be used in.

> *All parameters have local scope to the subroutine.*

> <u>Local variables</u> can only be used <u>within the structure</u> they're declared in — they have a <u>local scope</u>.
> <u>Global variables</u> can be used <u>any time</u> after their declaration — they have a <u>global scope</u>.

2) Variables declared inside a <u>subroutine</u> are <u>local variables</u>. They are <u>invisible</u> to the rest of the program — this means that they can't be used <u>outside</u> the subroutine.

3) The <u>advantage</u> of local variables is that their scope only extends to the subroutine they're declared in. They <u>can't affect</u> and are <u>not affected</u> by anything outside of the subroutine. It also doesn't matter if you use the <u>same variable name</u> as a local variable defined elsewhere in the program.

4) Variables in the <u>main body</u> of a program can be made into global variables using the 'GLOBAL' keyword — these variables can then be used anywhere in the program. It can be difficult to keep track of the <u>value</u> of global variables in <u>larger programs</u>.

5) The example below shows how <u>global variables</u> are used to store data outside of the subroutine.

x and y are defined <u>globally</u> — if they were declared inside the subroutine then they'd <u>reset to 0</u> each time the subroutine was called.

The subroutine is a <u>procedure</u> as it <u>doesn't</u> return a value.

The <u>parameters</u> a and b are added to the <u>global variables</u> x and y.

The program <u>keeps track</u> of the position after the first move and then applies the second move from that position.

```
# A subroutine to keep track of a character's x and y position.
GLOBAL x ← 0
GLOBAL y ← 0
SUBROUTINE move(a, b)
    x ← x + a
    y ← y + b
    OUTPUT '(' + INT_TO_STRING(x) + ', ' + INT_TO_STRING(y) + ')'
ENDSUBROUTINE
move(3, 5)
move(4, 7)
```

<u>a</u> and <u>b</u> are parameters so they have <u>local scope</u> to this procedure — they're <u>invisible</u> elsewhere in the program.

```
(3, 5)
(7, 12)
```

Sorry you can't come in, this function is for local variables only...

Subroutines are great at simplifying code and writing code in an efficient way. It's best to give variables a local scope wherever possible — that way you don't have to worry about them in the rest of your program.

Programming in Python®

In your exam, you'll need to know how to do everything covered on pages 8-22 using your chosen programming language. The next few pages will show you how to do it all using Python (version 3).

> If you're studying C# or VB.NET instead of Python, you can find similar pages for those languages in the online edition of this book.

1) Python code can typically be written in two places — the Python interactive shell (or console) or in a Python script file.

> On pages 23-27, Python code will be shown in these green boxes.
>
> Any output to the screen will be shown in these white boxes.

2) The interactive shell is useful for entering single commands or short blocks of code and running them immediately — it's great for debugging and getting used to Python basics.

3) Python script (.py) files are written using a text or code editor. They're useful for making programs you can save, edit and run multiple times. When you run a script file, the outputs are shown in the interactive shell.

The Data Type of a Variable is set Automatically

Nothing to declare

1) In Python, you can assign a value to a variable using the = operator. Variables don't need to be declared before you use them — they're created when you first assign a value to them.

2) The data type of a variable is set automatically according to the value assigned:

- Whole numbers without a decimal point will be assigned as integers.
- Any number with a decimal point will be assigned as a float.
- Anything inside quotation marks will be assigned as a string.
- The (case-sensitive) values True and False are assigned as Booleans.

> Strings can be written inside single or double quotation marks — just make sure you're consistent throughout your code.

3) If the variable is reassigned with a new value, it will take the data type of that new value.

Python has functions for Inputs, Outputs and Casting

1) Inputs from and outputs to the user all happen in the Python shell.

2) You can prompt the user to input data with the input() function. The string to display to the user asking them for an input goes inside the brackets.

```python
favNo = input("What's your favourite number? ")
print(favNo + " is a rubbish number.")
```

```
What's your favourite number? 21
21 is a rubbish number.
```

3) Anything you output using the print() function will be displayed on screen as text. Don't forget the brackets — it won't work without them.

4) The three main casting functions you need to know are str(), int() and float(). The data type that they convert to is clear from the function name, but they will only convert values given in the right form.

Function	Works on:
str()	Any data type.
int()	Whole number strings (e.g. "12") and floats (returns only the whole number part, e.g. int(12.8) will return 12).
float()	Integers (e.g. 12 converts to 12.0) and strings with only numbers and a decimal point (e.g. "12" and "12.0" both convert to 12.0).

```python
myInput = input("Enter a number. ")
print(myInput * 2)
intInput = int(myInput)
print(intInput * 2)
```

```
Enter a number. 32
3232      This didn't multiply by 2 because myInput is
64        a string — it needs to be cast as an integer.
```

5) When you assign a value to a variable using the input() function, it will always be a string. You can use casting to convert it to something more useful.

Don't feel constricted — with Python the possibilities are endless...

Once you get the hang of it, you'll be able to write code that does almost anything. Focus on learning the basics now, and you'll be casting integers to strings like some kind of data type wizard in no time.

Programming in Python®

Most operators are the same in Python as in AQA pseudo-code, but a few are slightly different, so take care.

Function	Operator
Addition	+
Subtraction	–
Multiplication	*
Division	/
Integer division	//
Remainder	%

Look out for Integer Division and Remainders

1) Almost all of the arithmetic operators in Python match the table on p9.

2) All of these operators will work on both integers and floats. However, the // and % operator should generally only be used on integer values — using them with floats can give unexpected results.

The Boolean Operators are Case-Sensitive

1) The comparison operators in Python are also similar to the ones on p9.

Operator	Meaning
==	Equal to
!=	Not equal to
<	Less than
>	Greater than
<=	Less than or equal to
>=	Greater than or equal to

2) "=" is the assignment operator, so Python uses "==" to compare if two expressions are equal.

3) There are no "≠", "≤" or "≥" keys on a standard keyboard, so Python uses what's available. For example, "less than or equal to" is a combination of less than (<) and equals (=).

4) In Python, the Boolean operators are 'and', 'not' and 'or'. These are case-sensitive — they should be all lower case.

5) Comparison operators can be used with Boolean operators, just like the examples on p16.

Python has lots of String Functions and Methods

> A 'method' is similar to a function, except it's written string.method rather than function(string).

1) On p11, you saw a few ways of manipulating strings. Python has equivalents of all of these, plus many more. Note that strings are indexed starting at 0.

Python Code	Operation
`len(string)`	Returns the number of characters in the string.
`string.index(substring)`	Returns the position of the first occurrence of a certain substring in the given string.
`string[x]`	Extracts the character at position x from the string.
`string[x:y]`	Extracts a substring from the original string starting at position x, up to but not including position y.
`string.upper()`	Returns the string in uppercase.
`string.lower()`	Returns the string in lowercase.
`string.isdigit()`	Returns True if the string contains only digits or False otherwise

```
petName = "Nibbles"
print(len(petName))
print(petName.upper())
print(petName.index("bb"))
print(petName[3:6])

7
NIBBLES     These are the characters
2           in positions 3, 4 and 5.
ble
```

2) You can concatenate strings with the + operator — this works exactly like the examples on p11.

3) If you want to print a mix of strings and other data types (e.g. integers), you can use commas to separate them. The advantage of this is that you don't have to cast everything as a string. It also automatically separates the values with spaces (by default).

```
age = 15
print("I am " + str(age) + " years old.")
print("I've been around for", age, "years.")

I am 15 years old.
I've been around for 15 years.
```

4) Python uses the functions ord() and chr() for converting characters to and from ASCII/Unicode® codes.

```
print(ord("Q"))    81
print(chr(99))     c
```

My code always works — I'm a smooth operator...

A lot of this might seem like stuff you've already seen, but don't get lazy. Using the wrong operators can create bugs in your code, so paying close attention now could save you a lot of time in the future...

Programming in Python®

Want to group lots of data together? Well, I have just the thing for you. Python has data structures that are similar to the arrays and records from p18-20 but with some key differences — including brand new names...

Lists have all the main features of Arrays

1) A list is a data structure in Python that is similar to an array.

2) Making a list follows the same process as creating an array on p18 — as usual, there's no need to declare anything before you start.

```
vowels = ["a","e","i","o","u"]
print(vowels[1])
print(len(vowels))
```
```
e
5
```

3) Unlike arrays, lists in Python allow you to store different data types in them, though you might want to use a dictionary (see below) for that instead.

4) The len(list) function tells you how many items are in the list. The position of each item is numbered starting from 0.

5) In a two-dimensional list, the position of each item is described using two sets of square brackets:

```
twoDList = [[1, 2, 3], [4, 5, 6], [7, 8, 9]]
print(twoDList[1])
print(twoDList[2][0])
```
```
[4, 5, 6]
7
```

6) There are other useful methods you can use with lists — for example, you can use append(item) to add an item to the end of a list, or pop(position of item) to remove an item from a specific position.

Dictionaries are the closest thing to Records in Python

1) A dictionary is another data structure in Python — it stores data together in key:value pairs.

2) The key is like the field name in a record, and the value is the data stored in that field. In this example, the key "Maths" has a corresponding value of 74.

Notice that dictionaries use curly brackets.

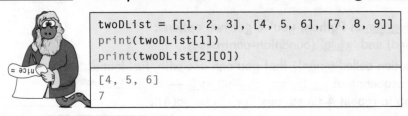

```
results = {"English":"C", "Maths":74, "Boolean Logic":True}
```

3) The keys will often be strings as these are the most useful for giving them descriptive names. The values can take any data type.

4) You can retrieve or edit a value by using the dictionary name and the key. You can also add new values by using a key that hasn't already been assigned, or delete a value using the keyword del.

```
print(results["Maths"])
results["English"] = "B"
results["Music"] = "A"
print(len(results))
del results["Boolean Logic"]
print(results)
```
```
74
4
{'English': 'B', 'Maths': 74,
'Music': 'A'}
```

5) To create lots of dictionaries with the same structure, you need to manually re-enter the same keys each time. You can collect these dictionaries in a list or in another dictionary — this is a really useful way of keeping all of the data organised.

```
results = {"Hifumi":{"English":"B", "Maths":74, "Music":"A"},
           "Cory":{"English":"C", "Maths":76, "Music":"Bb"},
           "June":{"English":"C", "Maths":61, "Music":"A#"}}
print(results["June"])
print(results["Cory"]["Music"])
```
```
{'English': 'C', 'Maths': 61, 'Music': 'A#'}
Bb
```

We've indented the code here so it's a bit easier to read.

My key:value pairs — door:52, car:36, lime pie:2674...

Lists and dictionaries in Python are quite flexible compared to data structures in other programming languages. You can add, remove and replace items, and also store different data types in the same data structure.

Programming in Python®

Python only has some of the selection and iteration statements covered on pages 12-15. One of the most important things about these statements is that they rely on indentation to specify where they start and end.

Indentation is Crucial in Python

1) <u>if</u>, <u>if-else</u> and <u>if-elif</u> (short for else if) are the <u>selection statements</u> in Python.

2) You don't need to tell them where to stop — instead, Python uses <u>indentation</u> to <u>work out</u> what code is supposed to be '<u>inside</u>' the statement.

3) You also need to put a <u>colon</u> : at the <u>end</u> of <u>each condition</u> you want to check.

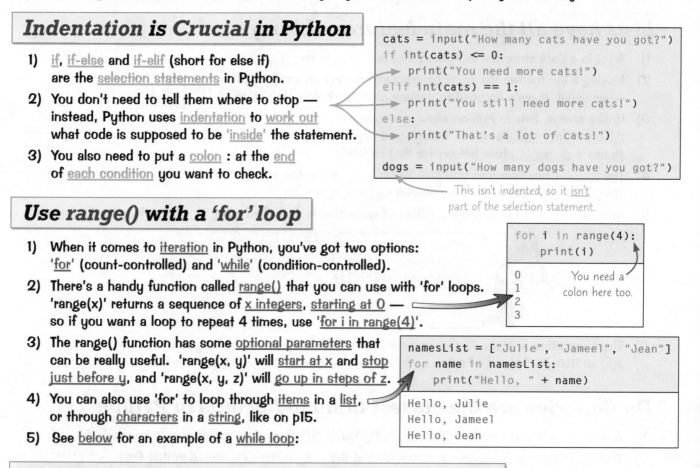

```
cats = input("How many cats have you got?")
if int(cats) <= 0:
    print("You need more cats!")
elif int(cats) == 1:
    print("You still need more cats!")
else:
    print("That's a lot of cats!")

dogs = input("How many dogs have you got?")
```

This isn't indented, so it <u>isn't</u> part of the selection statement.

Use range() with a 'for' loop

1) When it comes to <u>iteration</u> in Python, you've got two options: '<u>for</u>' (count-controlled) and '<u>while</u>' (condition-controlled).

2) There's a handy function called <u>range()</u> that you can use with 'for' loops. 'range(x)' returns a sequence of <u>x integers</u>, <u>starting at 0</u> — so if you want a loop to repeat 4 times, use '<u>for i in range(4)</u>'.

3) The range() function has some <u>optional parameters</u> that can be really useful. 'range(x, y)' will <u>start at x</u> and <u>stop just before y</u>, and 'range(x, y, z)' will <u>go up in steps of z</u>.

4) You can also use 'for' to loop through <u>items</u> in a <u>list</u>, or through <u>characters</u> in a <u>string</u>, like on p15.

5) See <u>below</u> for an example of a <u>while loop</u>:

```
for i in range(4):
    print(i)

0
1
2
3
```

You need a colon here too.

```
namesList = ["Julie", "Jameel", "Jean"]
for name in namesList:
    print("Hello, " + name)

Hello, Julie
Hello, Jameel
Hello, Jean
```

Use Nested Statements for Complex Programs

EXAMPLE: Write a program in Python code that takes an integer input from the user, then carries out a binary search for that number in an ordered list of integers called items.

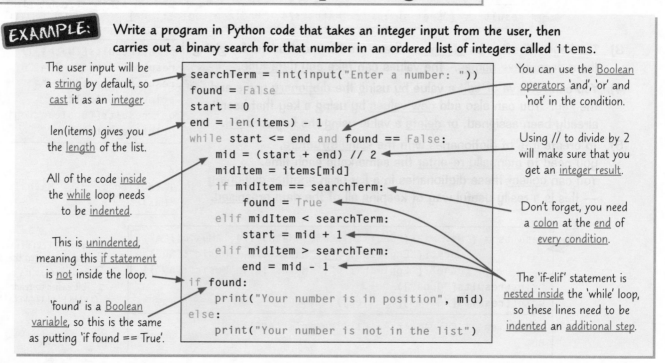

The user input will be a <u>string</u> by default, so <u>cast</u> it as an <u>integer</u>.

len(items) gives you the <u>length</u> of the list.

All of the code <u>inside</u> the <u>while</u> loop needs to be <u>indented</u>.

This is <u>unindented</u>, meaning this <u>if statement</u> is <u>not</u> inside the loop.

'found' is a <u>Boolean variable</u>, so this is the same as putting 'if found == True'.

```
searchTerm = int(input("Enter a number: "))
found = False
start = 0
end = len(items) - 1
while start <= end and found == False:
    mid = (start + end) // 2
    midItem = items[mid]
    if midItem == searchTerm:
        found = True
    elif midItem < searchTerm:
        start = mid + 1
    elif midItem > searchTerm:
        end = mid - 1
if found:
    print("Your number is in position", mid)
else:
    print("Your number is not in the list")
```

You can use the <u>Boolean operators</u> 'and', 'or' and 'not' in the condition.

Using // to divide by 2 will make sure that you get an <u>integer result</u>.

Don't forget, you need a <u>colon</u> at the <u>end</u> of <u>every condition</u>.

The 'if-elif' statement is <u>nested inside</u> the 'while' loop, so these lines need to be <u>indented</u> an <u>additional step</u>.

Not writing good Python code can have unindented consequences...

...but after enough practice, proper indentation will come as second nature. Just remember the golden rule — like a healthy digestive system, that colon is absolutely essential for keeping things running properly.

Programming in Python®

The last bit of Python knowledge I need to impart upon you is all about subroutines — see p21-22 if you need a recap. Just like that page reference, they stop you from having to write the same thing more than once.

Use *def* to create new *Subroutines in Python*

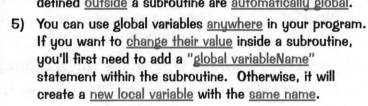

triple is a function because it returns a value — see p21.

```
def triple(number):
    result = number * 3
    return result

print(triple(4))
```
```
12
```

1) In Python, all subroutines are <u>defined</u> using the keyword '<u>def</u>'. You need to give your subroutine a <u>name</u>, define any <u>parameters</u> it takes and then use a <u>colon</u>. All the code you want in your subroutine should be <u>indented</u>.

2) You need to define subroutines <u>before</u> you use them, so it's usually a good idea to put all your definitions <u>at the start</u> of your program.

3) Values can be returned from subroutines using '<u>return</u>'. Like on p21, when you call a function, you need to <u>assign</u> it to a <u>variable</u>, otherwise the value it returns will be <u>lost</u>.

Inside the subroutine, 'animal' is a local variable, so its value is "Lion".

Outside the subroutine, 'animal' still has the value "Dog".

```
animal = "Dog"
def changeAnimal():
    animal = "Lion"
    print(animal)

changeAnimal()
print(animal)
```
```
Lion
Dog
```

4) In Python, any <u>variables</u> defined <u>inside</u> a subroutine will be <u>local variables</u> to that subroutine, while variables defined <u>outside</u> a subroutine are <u>automatically global</u>.

5) You can use global variables <u>anywhere</u> in your program. If you want to <u>change their value</u> inside a subroutine, you'll first need to add a "<u>global variableName</u>" statement within the subroutine. Otherwise, it will create a <u>new local variable</u> with the <u>same name</u>.

You can *Import Modules* into your *Program*

1) <u>Modules</u> are external <u>Python files</u> which often contain functions. Python has lots of <u>pre-existing</u> modules which you can take advantage of, so you don't have to write everything from scratch.

2) In order to use a module in your code, you use the '<u>import</u>' command along with the module's <u>name</u>. You should do this <u>at the very start</u> of your program.

3) To <u>call a function</u>, you'll need to write it in the form "<u>module.function</u>".

4) In Python, you need to use the '<u>random</u>' module to do <u>random number generation</u>. Once you've imported it, you can generate a <u>random integer</u> between two values x and y using the function <u>random.randint(x, y)</u>.

> You can also import a <u>specific</u> function from a module by writing "<u>from module import function</u>" — if you do this, you <u>don't</u> need to write "module." before the function when you call it.

```
import random                              The 'random' module is imported
                                           at the start of the program.
def pickACard():
    valueList = ["ace","2","3","4","5","6","7","8","9","10","jack",queen","king"]
    suitList = ["hearts", "spades", "diamonds", "clubs"]
    x = random.randint(0, 12)              x and y are assigned random values.
    y = random.randint(0, 3)              E.g. y could be either 0, 1, 2 or 3.
    card = valueList[x] + " of " + suitList[y]
    return card                This is a function because
                               it returns a value.
print(pickACard())                          Remember, you need to do something with the returned
print(pickACard())              value of the function after you call it — here we've printed it.
```
```
5 of diamonds          Because the values of x and y are randomly generated each time,
jack of hearts         the results are likely to be different every time the function is called.
```

5) The random module also has <u>other useful functions</u>. For example, <u>random.uniform(x, y)</u> generates a random <u>float</u> rather than an integer, and <u>random.choice(list)</u> picks a random item from a list (this could have been used in the example above).

This page is def my fav in the whole book...

Modules might sound complicated, but they're incredibly useful. As well as saving you lots of time writing your own functions, they also tend to be more reliable than code you've written yourself (no offence).

Revision Questions for Section Two

Well, that just about wraps up the programming section — perfect time to try some revision questions I think.

- Try these questions and <u>tick off each one</u> when you <u>get it right</u>.
- When you've done <u>all the questions</u> for a topic and are <u>completely happy</u> with it, tick off the topic.

Data Types, Operators, Constants, Variables and Strings (p8-11) ☑

1) Define the following data types: integer, real, Boolean, character and string.

2)* Write a piece of pseudo-code that converts:
   a) the string '1234' into an integer.   b) the real 0.578 into a string.
   c) the integer 8 into a string.   d) the string '0.75' into a real.

3) In AQA pseudo-code, what do each of these operators do?
   a) =   b) MOD   c) *   d) ←   e) DIV

4) What is meant by: a) a constant?   b) a variable?

5) a) Define string concatenation and give an example of it being used.
   b)* What will each of the following pieces of pseudo-code return if colour ← 'magenta'?
      (i) LEN(colour)   (ii) POSITION(colour, 'g')   (iii) SUBSTRING(0, 3, colour)

Program Flow, Boolean Operators and Random Numbers (p12-17) ☑

6) In 20 words or less, outline what each of these statements does:
   a) IF statement   b) CASE statement.

7) What is the main difference between ELSE-IF statements and nested IF statements?

8) Compare the features of the three condition-controlled loops, REPEAT-UNTIL, WHILE and DO-WHILE.

9)* Write an algorithm that outputs the number of Mondays in a 30-day month
   when the user inputs the day of the week that the month started on.

10)* Write an algorithm to simulate 100 rolls of an 8-sided dice and output the result of each roll.

Arrays, Records and Subroutines (p18-22) ☑

11) Why are arrays useful?

12)* Write commands to perform the following operations on this array. The name of the array is 'chars'.
   ['3', 'T', 'P', '2', 'M', 'e', '4', 'q', 's', '3'].
   a) Output the character 'M'.   b) Replace the 'P' in the chars array with a 'D'.
   c) Replace every element in the chars array with an 'N'.

13)* Write an algorithm to create a two-dimensional array with 10 rows and 10 columns where each
   element is an integer and its value is given by the row number multiplied by the column number.
   (Hint: Remember that rows and columns are numbered starting at 0.)

14) In programming, data can be stored in records:
   a) What is a record?   b) Give two differences between a record and a field.

15) What is a subroutine?

16) What is the difference between a function and a procedure?

17) Define these terms: a) parameter   b) local variable   c) global variable

Programming in Python® (p23-27) ☐

18) Explain how input() and print() work in Python.

19) What are the three main casting functions in Python?

20) List three different string functions/methods.

21) Describe the features of these Python data structures: a) list   b) dictionary

22)* Write two Python subroutines that take a string as a parameter and print it 10 times.
   Each of your subroutines should use a different type of iteration statement.

                                    *Answers on p80

Structured Programming

On p21-22 you saw how subroutines could be used to store a whole set of instructions under one name. Well, a single program will typically use lots of subroutines that each perform specific and simple tasks.

Structured Programming makes Coding much Easier

1) Structured (or modular) programming involves decomposing (see p1) the program that you want to write into manageable modules. Each of those modules is then decomposed even further into smaller modules and eventually into modules that perform individual tasks.

2) Simple subroutines can be written to carry out each individual task. Then the bigger modules and main program can be written using these subroutines.

3) It's important to clearly document the interface of each module. This means listing the module's name, any inputs (i.e. parameters), processes (what the module does) and the output/return value (if any).

4) For example, to design a program simulating a game of noughts and crosses you might have:

Program module design

Noughts and Crosses Program
- Set up a new game
  - Enter player names
  - Enter number of rounds
  - Choose who goes first
- Play the game
- Work out winner
- Reset the program

Module interface for setting up a new game

Module	Input(s)	Process	Return Value
Enter player names	None	Prompt user for two names	Array of player names
Enter number of rounds	None	Prompt user for a number of rounds	Number of rounds
Choose who goes first	Array of player names	Randomly select a name	Name of player going first

The output of one module is often the input of another.

ADVANTAGES OF STRUCTURED PROGRAMMING

- Coding is easier because you're only writing subroutines that carry out very simple tasks.
- Lots of programmers can work on one program as each module can be written independently.
- It's easier to test structured programs as each module can be tested individually (see p31).
- Individual subroutines and modules can be fixed and updated without affecting the rest of the program.
- You will be able to reuse the subroutines and modules in programs you write in the future.

Your program should be Easy To Maintain

1) When using structured programming, it's important that your code is well-maintained.

2) A well-maintained program makes it easy for other programmers to understand what the code does. They should also be able to change parts of the source code without the risk of causing problems elsewhere in the code (e.g. knock on effects).

3) The following features can improve the maintainability of source code:

- Comments (usually written after # or //) are useful for explaining what the key features of a program do — well written and clear comments are fundamental for helping other programmers understand your programs.

  Too many comments can leave your programs looking cluttered and unreadable.

- Indentation can be used to separate different statements in a program. This allows other programmers to see the flow of the program more clearly and pick out the different features.

- Variables, subroutines and parameters should be named so that they refer to what they actually are. This helps programmers to understand what they do, and makes it easier to keep track of them.

- Only use global variables (see p22) when necessary as they could affect the rest of your code. Variables with a local scope will only affect the subroutines that they are declared in — other programmers will know that changing these variables won't affect other parts of the program.

Look after your programs and they will look after you...

The key to a well-structured program is plenty of planning — decomposing the program into modules is always the first step. Have a go at finishing off the design for the noughts and crosses program above.

Authentication and Validation

Authentication and validation are used to improve the security and robustness of your programs.

Authentication can help Protect your programs

1) <u>Authentication</u> can <u>confirm the identity</u> of a user before they're allowed to access certain pieces of data or features of the program. A common way that programs do this is using <u>passwords</u>.

2) <u>Passwords</u> are usually associated with a <u>username</u>. When someone tries to access a protected part of the program, it should ask them for their password to check that they are who they claim to be.

3) Here are some common ways to <u>increase the security</u> of a password-based authentication system:

> • Force users to use <u>strong passwords</u> (p72) and get them to change their passwords <u>regularly</u>.
> • Limit the number of <u>failed authentication attempts</u> before access to an account is lost.
> • Ask for a <u>random selection of characters</u> from the password on each authentication.

4) It's important that programmers get the <u>level of authentication</u> correct — too much authentication can affect a program's <u>functionality</u> and put people off using it.

5) A typical <u>authentication routine</u> will follow this structure:

Validation can make sure the Inputs can't be Exploited

1) The easiest way for a user to <u>accidentally</u> or <u>intentionally misuse</u> a program is when entering data. You can try to prevent this from happening by using <u>validation</u>.

> **INPUT VALIDATION** — checking if data meets <u>certain criteria</u> before passing it into the program.
> E.g. checking that an email address contains an @ symbol and has a suitable ending (.com, .co.uk, etc).

2) Here are a few common types of <u>input validation check</u> you can use:

Range check	Checks the data is within a <u>specified range</u>.
Presence check	Checks the data has actually been <u>entered</u>.
Format check	Checks the data has the <u>correct format</u> (e.g. a date).
Look-up table	Checks the data against a table of <u>acceptable values</u>.
Length check	Checks the data is the <u>correct length</u>.

EXAMPLE:

Karen wants to validate usernames for an online forum. She wants each username to be longer than 5 characters, shorter than 12 characters and start with an uppercase letter.

a) Give two validation checks Karen would need to use.
 • Length check to make sure the username is not longer or shorter than the lengths allowed.
 • Format check to make sure the username starts with an uppercase letter.

b) Write a subroutine that will check if a username is a valid length.

```
SUBROUTINE validateUsername(username)
    usernameLength ← LEN(username)
    IF usernameLength > 5 AND usernameLength < 12 THEN
        RETURN True
    ELSE
        RETURN False
    ENDIF
ENDSUBROUTINE
```

I'm taking my wife hiking at the weekend — it's our first validate...

You should be able to write subroutines to perform simple authentication and validation checks.
Think about who you want to access your programs and what data you want them to be able to enter.

Testing

When you're writing programs, remember that the testing is just as important as the programming itself. Have a look at this page to test your knowledge of testing — they'll prepare you for being tested in the tests.

Programming Errors can be *Syntax Errors* and *Logic Errors*

1) It's quite typical for a program to contain <u>errors</u> during its development — these errors need to be <u>found</u> and <u>corrected</u> as soon as possible.

2) The first task is to figure out what <u>type of error</u> has occurred:

> SYNTAX ERRORS — when the compiler or interpreter <u>doesn't understand</u> something you've typed because it doesn't follow the <u>rules</u> or <u>grammar</u> of the programming language.
>
> LOGIC ERRORS — when the compiler or interpreter is able to <u>run the program</u>, but the program does something <u>unexpected</u>.

3) <u>Syntax errors</u> can be <u>diagnosed</u> by compilers and interpreters (see p60) — they'll be unable to <u>translate</u> the <u>source code</u> and a syntax error (with its location) will be returned.

4) <u>Logic errors</u> are more <u>difficult to diagnose</u> and <u>track down</u> — compilers and interpreters <u>won't</u> pick them up. Logic errors are found through general use of the program and by systematically <u>testing</u> it using a <u>test plan</u> (see below).

You can't fault his logic but his syntax is all over the place.

A Test Plan *should be made* Before Implementation

1) A <u>test plan</u> will outline exactly what you're going to test and how you're going to test it. It should cover all the <u>possible paths</u> through a program.

Possible paths are all the branches of the flowchart (p3) for your program.

2) A <u>good test plan</u> will anticipate potential issues with the program and select appropriate <u>test data</u> to test for these issues.

3) The <u>test data</u> that you use in your test plan should fall into one of three categories:

- <u>Normal (typical) data</u> — <u>valid</u> data that a user is <u>likely</u> to input into the program.
- <u>Boundary (extreme) data</u> — <u>valid</u> or <u>invalid</u> data on <u>either side</u> of the <u>boundary</u> of what the program should accept.
- <u>Erroneous data</u> — invalid data that the program <u>should not accept</u>.

Extreme enough for ya?

4) The table below shows an example of a test plan for setting an alarm system. Users should be able to set their own **3-5 digit alarm code**.

Type of data	Test data	Reason for testing	Expected outcome
Normal	2476	To see how the alarm copes with normal usage.	Code accepted.
Boundary	000	To see if the smallest code is accepted.	Code accepted.
Boundary	99999	To see if the largest code is accepted.	Code accepted.
Boundary	100000	To see if a code that's just over the boundary is accepted.	Error: The code is too long.
Erroneous	23aY	To see if the system accepts non-digits.	Error: The code contains non-numeric data.
Erroneous	8	To see if the alarm accepts fewer than 3-digit inputs.	Error: The code is too short.
Erroneous	1134277	To see if the alarm accepts more than 5-digit inputs.	Error: The code is too long.

5) During testing, the tester can add "<u>actual outcome</u>" and "<u>pass or fail</u>" columns to the table.

6) <u>Trace tables</u> (see p32) can be used when you've <u>identified</u> that there is a logic error. They will help you <u>trace the values</u> that the variables take as you go through the program so you can <u>pin-point exactly</u> where something has <u>gone wrong</u>.

Sorry, this page is still in the testing stage... Error 50: Line is too long!

When it comes to your exams you'll need to be able to choose suitable test data for a given program — remember that you'll need to choose normal, boundary and erroneous data. A handy tip is to think "How could I ruin the programmer's day by breaking their beloved program?" and you'll be all set.

Trace Tables and Time Efficiency

Trace tables will be your best friend when you're learning the fundamentals of programming. They help you to follow a piece of code in a systematic way to see if it's behaving itself or if it's up to no good.

Trace Tables help you to find Logic Errors

1) Trace tables give a simple way of testing that a piece of code is working correctly. They keep track of the values that certain variables take as you go through the code.

2) Their main use is to 'dry run' a subroutine or algorithm to make sure there are no logic errors — they can also be used to help you figure out what a piece of code is actually doing.

3) The columns of a trace table usually represent variables. Each row of a trace table represents the values that the variables take at a particular point in the algorithm.

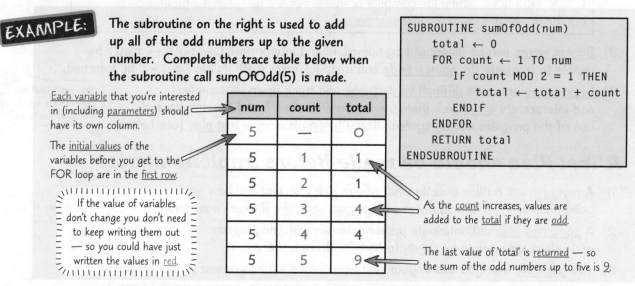

EXAMPLE: The subroutine on the right is used to add up all of the odd numbers up to the given number. Complete the trace table below when the subroutine call sumOfOdd(5) is made.

Each variable that you're interested in (including parameters) should have its own column.

The initial values of the variables before you get to the FOR loop are in the first row.

If the value of variables don't change you don't need to keep writing them out — so you could have just written the values in red.

num	count	total
5	—	0
5	1	1
5	2	1
5	3	4
5	4	4
5	5	9

```
SUBROUTINE sumOfOdd(num)
    total ← 0
    FOR count ← 1 TO num
        IF count MOD 2 = 1 THEN
            total ← total + count
        ENDIF
    ENDFOR
    RETURN total
ENDSUBROUTINE
```

As the count increases, values are added to the total if they are odd.

The last value of 'total' is returned — so the sum of the odd numbers up to five is 9.

4) The columns of a trace table might not always be variables — they could be any information that the programmer is interested in. For example, they might have a column for the length of an array or for the output of the algorithm.

5) When testing a larger program, the tester will often use debugging tools — for example, breakpoints are used to stop the program at certain places so that you can look at the values of variables.

Table tracing attempt #9

Algorithms are also tested for Time Efficiency

1) Many different algorithms can be constructed to perform the same task (e.g. the searching and sorting algorithms on p4-6).

2) Each algorithm will take a certain amount of 'time' to complete the task. Algorithms that take less 'time' to complete a task are said to have a better time efficiency.

3) When programmers talk about the amount of 'time' an algorithm takes, they usually don't measure the real-life time. They measure things like the number of times memory was accessed, the number of CPU cycles taken to execute commands or the number of times a loop was executed.

```
SUBROUTINE sumOfOdd(num)
    n ← (num + 1) DIV 2
    total ← n * n
    RETURN total
ENDSUBROUTINE
```

This subroutine does exactly the same as the one above but it doesn't have a loop. For large values of the parameter this algorithm would have a much better time efficiency.

Programmers are often interested in the space efficiency of an algorithm too — this is the amount of space in memory that an algorithm uses.

How many times did you access memory on that page?

Time efficient revision isn't always best — sometimes you just need to keep looping through a page until you remember it. If trace tables crop up in your exam, you might not be told the purpose of the algorithm you're tracing — don't worry, just work your way through the algorithm pretending you're a computer.

Revision Questions for Section Three

And just like that it's the end of <u>Section Three</u> — but before you put the book down, you've got one more task.

- Try these questions and <u>tick off each one</u> when you <u>get it right</u>.
- When you've done <u>all the questions</u> for a topic and are <u>completely happy</u> with it, tick off the topic.

Structured Programming, Authentication and Validation (p29-30) ☑

1) What is structured programming?
2) Give five advantages of using structured programming.
3) a) Give four features of maintainable source code.
   b) Explain how each feature can help other programmers to maintain your code.
4) What is authentication and why is it used?
5) Give three things that can be done to make a password-based authentication system more secure.
6) Draw a flowchart to show a standard username and password authentication routine.
7) Define the term input validation.
8) Give five types of input validation check and explain what each check does.
9)* The program below checks which year the user was born in.
   What type of input validation check does it use? Explain your answer.

```
REPEAT
    OUTPUT 'Enter the year you were born'
    year ← USERINPUT
UNTIL year > 1900 AND year <= 2016
```

Testing (p31) ☑

10) Define the following terms:　　a) Syntax Error　　b) Logic Error
11) Explain why logic errors are more difficult to diagnose than syntax errors.
12)*This algorithm should take the user's age and output a message based on their age.
    Find two errors in the code and suggest ways that you could fix them.

```
age ← USERINPUT
ageString ← INT_TO_STRING(age)
IF age > 16 THEN
    message ← 'At the age of ' + age + ' you must be a computer science genius'
ELSEIF age < 16 THEN
    message ← 'Practice makes perfect!'
ENDIF
OUTPUT message
```

13) What are the three different types of test data?
14)*A software company is designing an anagram application. It will take a string
    of letters and return all of the words that can be spelt using all of the letters exactly once.
    Come up with five pieces of test data that the company could use to test their program.

Trace Tables and Time Efficiency (p32) ☑

15) What are trace tables used for?
16)*Complete the trace table for the algorithm given on the right. You may need to add more rows.

```
arr ← [2, 5, 1, 2, 3]
total ← 1
FOR x ← 0 TO LEN(arr)-1
    total ← total * arr[x]
ENDFOR
OUTPUT total
```

x	arr[x]	total

17) Describe what time efficiency is in the most time efficient way possible.

*Answers on p81

Section Three — Design and Testing

Logic

Logic gates are pretty clever — they take binary information and give an output based on the Boolean operations (p16). Each Boolean operation (<u>NOT</u>, <u>AND</u>, <u>OR</u>) has its own logic gate, plus you've got a new friend called <u>XOR</u>.

Logic Gates *apply* Boolean Operations *to* Inputs

1) Logic gates are special circuits built into computer chips.
   They receive <u>binary data</u>, apply a <u>Boolean operation</u>, then <u>output</u> a binary result.

2) Logic <u>diagrams</u> are often drawn to show logic gates and circuits.
   Each type of logic gate is shown by a different <u>symbol</u>.

   It can help to think of 1s as TRUE and 0s as FALSE.

3) Each type of logic gate also has a corresponding <u>truth table</u>.
   Truth tables show <u>all</u> possible input combinations of 1s and 0s, and the corresponding <u>outputs</u>.

NOT gate

1) NOT gates take a <u>single input</u> and give a <u>single output</u>.

2) The output is always the <u>opposite</u> value to the input.
   If <u>1</u> is input, it outputs <u>0</u>.
   If <u>0</u> is input, it outputs <u>1</u>.

Input	Output
0	1
1	0

NOT gate symbol

Input ——▷o—— Output

AND gate

1) AND gates take <u>two inputs</u> and give <u>one output</u>.

2) If both inputs are 1, the output is <u>1</u>, <u>otherwise</u> the output is <u>0</u>.

Input A	Input B	Output
0	0	0
0	1	0
1	0	0
1	1	1

AND gate symbol

Input A ——⊐
)—— Output
Input B ——⊐

OR gate

Input A	Input B	Output
0	0	0
0	1	1
1	0	1
1	1	1

1) OR gates take <u>two inputs</u> and give <u>one output</u>.

2) If <u>one or more</u> inputs are 1, then the output is <u>1</u>, <u>otherwise</u> the output is <u>0</u>.

OR gate symbol

Input A ——⊃
)—— Output
Input B ——⊃

XOR gate

1) XOR gates take <u>two inputs</u> and give <u>one output</u>.

2) If <u>exactly one</u> input is 1, then the output is <u>1</u>, <u>otherwise</u> the output is <u>0</u>.

Input A	Input B	Output
0	0	0
0	1	1
1	0	1
1	1	0

XOR gate symbol

Input A ——⊃
)—— Output
Input B ——⊃

XOR is short for 'exclusive OR'.

Logic isn't as scary as it looks...

These basic logic gates are the building blocks for bigger logic circuits — which you'll see over the next couple of pages. You should be able to draw each logic gate, as well as the corresponding truth table.

Logic

You can make more interesting logic diagrams by combining logic gates. If you know the truth tables from the previous page you'll be able to create truth tables for much more complicated logic diagrams.

Logic Gates are Combined for More Complex Operations

1) Multiple logic gates can be added to the same logic circuit to carry out different operations.

2) You can work out the truth tables by working through each gate in order.
   For every input combination, follow them through each gate step-by-step, then write down the output.

3) By using brackets and the terms NOT, AND, OR and XOR, circuits can be written as logical statements, like NOT(A AND B) below. Operations in brackets should be completed first, just like in normal maths.

This circuit shows AND followed by NOT.

Input A
Input B
Output P

The truth table looks like this:

A	B	A AND B	P = NOT(A AND B)
0	0	0	1
0	1	0	1
1	0	0	1
1	1	1	0

This circuit shows XOR followed by NOT.

Input C
Input D
Output Q

The truth table looks like this:

C	D	C XOR D	Q = NOT(C XOR D)
0	0	0	1
0	1	1	0
1	0	1	0
1	1	0	1

4) The two logic circuits shown above are examples of two-level logic circuits — they require the inputs to pass through a maximum of two logic gates to reach the output.

Logic Circuits can have More than Two Inputs

This is a two-level logic circuit with 3 inputs.

Using Boolean operations, this circuit can be written as (A OR B) AND (NOT C).

Input A
Input B
Output R
Input C

To cover every input combination, extra rows are needed in the truth table. There are 3 inputs and each can take one of 2 values, so $2 \times 2 \times 2 = 8$ rows are needed.

In general, the number of rows is 2^n, where n is the number of different inputs.

A	B	C	A OR B	NOT C	R = (A OR B) AND (NOT C)
0	0	0	0	1	0
0	0	1	0	0	0
0	1	0	1	1	1
0	1	1	1	0	0
1	0	0	1	1	1
1	0	1	1	0	0
1	1	0	1	1	1
1	1	1	1	0	0

To be OR NOT to be — literally covering all forms of being...

Once you've learned each gate's truth table, you can work out the truth tables of much more complicated circuits. If you take the inputs through each gate one step at a time you'll be fine — it's only logical...

Logic

You might also see logic statements written using Boolean expression operators. You need to be able to write and interpret Boolean expressions using these operators, but once you learn what the symbols mean, you'll be flying.

There are *Symbols* for each *Boolean Operator*

1) Each of the logic operations, <u>NOT</u>, <u>AND</u>, <u>OR</u> and <u>XOR</u>, can also be written using a <u>symbol</u> (operator).

Operation	NOT A	A AND B	A OR B	A XOR B
Symbol	$\overline{A}$	A . B	A + B	A ⊕ B

2) You can use these symbols to describe <u>logic circuits</u> as well. <u>Brackets</u> work in the same way that they do for expressions written in <u>words</u> — so (A OR B) XOR C can be written (A + B) ⊕ C in symbols.

3) The <u>bar</u> for **NOT** should <u>extend</u> over <u>everything</u> it applies to — so NOT(D OR E) would be written $\overline{(D + E)}$.

MegaXORd Activated!

You can *Convert* between *Symbols* and *Words*

An exam question could give you a <u>logic statement</u> made up of those <u>symbols</u> and ask you to draw a <u>logic circuit diagram</u> and/or <u>truth table</u> for the expression.

EXAMPLE: Draw a logic circuit and truth table for the Boolean expression below.

$$T = \overline{A} + (B . C)$$

1) Start by writing the expression in <u>words</u>: $\overline{A}$ means <u>NOT A</u>, and (B . C) means <u>B AND C</u>. + means OR, so the whole expression means <u>(NOT A) OR (B AND C)</u>.

2) It's helpful to have <u>columns</u> for (NOT A) and for (B AND C) in the truth table.

3) The <u>logic circuit diagram</u> looks like this:

Input A — Input B — Input C — — Output T

A	B	C	$\overline{A}$	B . C	T = $\overline{A}$ + (B . C)
0	0	0	1	0	1
0	0	1	1	0	1
0	1	0	1	0	1
0	1	1	1	1	1
1	0	0	0	0	0
1	0	1	0	0	0
1	1	0	0	0	0
1	1	1	0	1	1

EXAMPLE: A machine in a factory uses a logic circuit for a safety mechanism. It receives two inputs, F and G, from two buttons, and the machine will only activate if exactly one of the buttons is turned on. There is also a safety switch, input H — the machine will only activate if H is switched on.

Create a Boolean expression to represent this safety mechanism.

1) The machine requires <u>exactly one</u> of the buttons to be pressed, so this means <u>F XOR G</u>.

2) It <u>also</u> needs H to be true, which means it's <u>this AND H</u>.

(F XOR G) AND H

or, in symbols: (F ⊕ G) . H

Alright — I've mastered the snare, the toms and the bass drum...

...so now it's time to learn the symbols. Once you get in the rhythm, you'll find these questions much easier. Make sure you're happy drawing logic circuit diagrams and truth tables for a given logic statement.

Units

Just like you have units like centimetres, metres and kilometres for measuring distance, computers need units for measuring <u>digital information</u>. It looks like whoever came up with them was really hungry at the time...

Bits are the Smallest Measure of Data

1) Computers use 1s and 0s to represent the flow of electricity.
   <u>1</u> is used to show that electricity <u>is</u> flowing, and <u>0</u> shows that it is <u>not</u> flowing.

2) All the data we want a computer to process must be converted into <u>binary code</u> (1s and 0s).

3) Each 1 or 0 in a binary code is a <u>bit</u> (<u>bi</u>nary dig<u>it</u>). For example, 1010 is 4 bits.

4) The table below shows <u>the size</u> of other units of data:

A <u>byte</u> is big enough to store one <u>character</u> (like x, e, M or £). See p43 for more info.

Most <u>files</u> (like <u>songs</u>, <u>pictures</u> and <u>documents</u>) are measured in <u>kB</u> or <u>MB</u>.

High definition <u>videos</u> and complex <u>applications</u> are often measured in <u>gigabytes</u>.

<u>Secondary storage</u> capacity is measured in <u>gigabytes</u> or <u>terabytes</u>.

Name	Size
Bit (b)	A single binary digit (1 or 0)
Nibble	4 bits
Byte (B)	8 bits
Kilobyte (kB)	1000 bytes
Megabyte (MB)	1000 kilobytes
Gigabyte (GB)	1000 megabytes
Terabyte (TB)	1000 gigabytes

You might see each unit defined to be 1024 (not 1000) times bigger than the previous unit. The main reason is that 1024 is a power of 2 which is helpful when dealing with binary data.

5) Each <u>bit</u> can take one of <u>two different values</u> (either 1 or 0). This means that a <u>nibble</u> (4 bits) can take $2^4 = $ <u>16 different values</u>, and a <u>byte</u> (8 bits) can take $2^8 = $ <u>256 different values</u>.

You can Convert between Different Units

<u>Converting</u> between units of data is usually pretty straightforward — just watch out when you have to switch between <u>bits</u> and <u>bytes</u>.

EXAMPLE: Ashley has downloaded some images to her computer. Each image is 300 kilobytes.

a) How many bits are in each image?

1) First, convert to bytes by <u>multiplying by 1000</u>: 300 kB = 300 × 1000 = 300 000 Bytes

2) There are 8 bits in a byte, so <u>multiply by 8</u>: 300 000 Bytes = 300 000 × 8
   = 2 400 000 bits

b) She wants to copy 400 of these images onto her USB flash drive, which has 0.15 GB of free space left. Does she have enough space to store them all?

1) Work out the <u>total size</u> of all the images: 400 × 300 = 120 000 kB

2) Now convert this to GB — first, <u>divide by 1000</u> to get it in MB, then <u>again</u> to get it in GB: 120 000 kB = 120 000 ÷ 1000 = 120 MB
   120 MB = 120 ÷ 1000 = 0.12 GB

So yes, she has enough space.

This page has me in bits...

Keep working your way through that unit table until the size order is clear in your head — it might just show up on your exam. A bit is smaller than a nibble, and a nibble is less than a full byte. I know, hilarious.

Binary Numbers

As computers only understand 1s and 0s, all data must be converted into binary to be processed. Binary can be used to represent all numbers in our standard number system.

Counting in Binary is a bit like Counting in Decimal

1) In our standard number system we have ten different digits (0, 1, 2, 3, 4, 5, 6, 7, 8, 9). This is called <u>decimal</u>, <u>denary</u> or <u>base-10</u>.

2) <u>Binary</u> only uses <u>two</u> different digits (0 and 1) — we call this <u>base-2</u>.

3) Counting in binary is similar to counting in decimal, but the place values from <u>right</u> to <u>left</u> increase by <u>powers of 2</u> (e.g. 8, 4, 2, 1), instead of powers of 10 (e.g. 1000, 100, 10, 1).

4) The following table shows the <u>binary equivalents</u> of the <u>decimal numbers 0-15</u>:

0 = 0	4 = 100	8 = 1000	12 = 1100
1 = 1	5 = 101	9 = 1001	13 = 1101
2 = 10	6 = 110	10 = 1010	14 = 1110
3 = 11	7 = 111	11 = 1011	15 = 1111

Binary Numbers are easier to Convert using Tables

Drawing a table with binary <u>place values</u> in the first row makes binary to decimal conversion easier.

EXAMPLE: Convert the 8-bit binary number 0011 0101 to a decimal number.

1) Draw up a table with binary place values in the top row. Start with 1 at the right, then move left, doubling each time.

128	64	32	16	8	4	2	1
0	0	1	1	0	1	0	1

Each column is just a power of 2. i.e. 2^3, 2^2, 2^1, 2^0.

2) Write the binary number 0011 0101 into your table.

3) Add up all the numbers with a 1 in their column: $32 + 16 + 4 + 1 = 53$

So 0011 0101 is 53 in decimal.

This works with all binary numbers — just draw as many columns as you need, doubling each time.

<u>8-bit</u> numbers can represent the decimal numbers 0 to 255. <u>16-bit</u> numbers can show the numbers 0 to 65 535, and <u>32-bit</u> can show the numbers 0 to 4 294 967 295.

Convert Decimal to Binary by Subtracting

When converting from <u>decimal</u> to <u>binary</u>, it's easier to draw a <u>table</u> of binary place values, then <u>subtract them</u> from <u>largest</u> to <u>smallest</u>. Have a look at this example:

EXAMPLE: Convert the decimal number 79 into an 8-bit binary number.

1) Draw an 8-bit table.

128	64	32	16	8	4	2	1
0	1	0	0	1	1	1	1

2) Move along the table, <u>only</u> subtracting the number in each column from your <u>running total</u> if it gives a <u>positive</u> answer.

3) Put a 0 in every column that gives a negative answer, and a 1 in the rest.

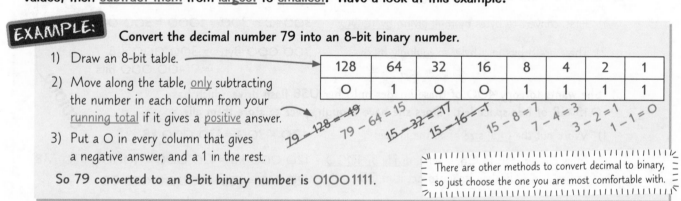

$79 - 128 = -49$ $79 - 64 = 15$ $15 - 32 = -17$ $15 - 16 = -1$ $15 - 8 = 7$ $7 - 4 = 3$ $3 - 2 = 1$ $1 - 1 = 0$

So 79 converted to an 8-bit binary number is 0100 1111.

There are other methods to convert decimal to binary, so just choose the one you are most comfortable with.

Why was 110 afraid of 111? Because 111 1000 1001...

There are a couple of different conversions on this page, and you'll need to be comfortable with it all before carrying on. Remember that to read each digit from smallest to largest, read from right to left like with decimal numbers. The value of each digit in binary is double the value of the digit to its right.

Binary Numbers

More binary numbers coming right up, hope you're ready for another page full of 0s and 1s. Adding binary numbers is a lot like adding decimal numbers — have a look at this page of examples to see how it's done...

Add Binary Numbers using Column Addition

As binary only uses 1s and 0s we <u>can</u> comfortably do 0 + 0 = 0, 1 + 0 = 1 and 0 + 1 = 1.

Using binary we <u>can't</u> write 1 + 1 = 2. Instead, we have to write <u>1 + 1 = 10</u>.

EXAMPLES: 1. Add the following 8-bit binary numbers together: 10001101 and 01001000

1) First, put the binary numbers into <u>columns</u>.

2) Starting from the <u>right</u>, add the numbers in columns.

3) When doing <u>1 + 1 = 10</u>, carry the 1 into the next column.

So 10001101 + 01001000 = 11010101

```
   1 0 0 0 1 1 0 1
 + 0 1 0 0 1 0 0 0
   1 1 0 1 0 1 0 1
               1
```

You can add <u>more binary numbers</u> together at the same time — just be careful when you get 1 + 1 + 1...

2. Calculate the sum of the binary numbers 01001011, 10001001 and 00100101.

```
    0 1 0 0 1 0 1 1
    1 0 0 0 1 0 0 1
  + 0 0 1 0 0 1 0 1
    1 1 1 1 1 0 0 1
        1 1 1 1
```

1) Put the numbers in <u>columns</u> and add from the <u>right</u> like before.

2) Sometimes you'll get something like <u>1 + 1 + 1 = 11</u>, so you need to write 1, then carry 1 to the next column.

So 01001011 + 10001001 + 00100101 = 11111001

You can add binary numbers with <u>different numbers of bits</u> — just <u>add some 0s</u> to the <u>front</u> of the numbers with fewer bits.

```
1 + 0 = 1
0 + 1 = 1
1 + 1 = 2̶ 10
1 + 1 + 1 = 3̶ 11
```

3. Calculate the sum of the binary numbers 110011, 1101001 and 10110

1) <u>Add zeros</u> to the front of 110011 and 10110 so that all the numbers have <u>7-bits</u>.

2) Add up the numbers in the normal way.

3) The answer has <u>8-bits</u>.

So 110011 + 1101001 + 10110 = 10110010

```
    0 1 1 0 0 1 1
    1 1 0 1 0 0 1
  + 0 0 1 0 1 1 0
  1 0 1 1 0 0 1 0
    1 1 1 1 1 1 1
```

You can <u>check your answers</u> to binary addition by converting the numbers and answer to <u>decimal</u>, to make sure it still works. For example 3 above:

110011 = 51   1101001 = 105

10110 = 22   10110010 = 178

51 + 105 + 22 = 178 so the answer is correct.

Binary Benefit #1010 — 10 Green Bottles is much shorter...

Okay, so that was a lot of examples just adding binary numbers together... But the best way to learn how to do it is practice, practice and more practice. You can test yourself by writing down two or three random binary numbers and adding them together, then check your answer by converting it all to decimal.

Binary Numbers

Computers have a few tricks to help them do tough calculations — one of these tricks is using binary shifts...

Binary Shifts can be used to Multiply or Divide by 2

1) A binary shift (also known as a logical shift) moves every bit in a binary number left or right a certain number of places.

2) Gaps at the beginning or end of the number are filled in with 0s.

3) The direction of the binary shift indicates whether it multiplies or divides the binary number:

Left shifts MULTIPLY a binary number.
For every place shifted left, the number is doubled.

Right shifts DIVIDE a binary number.
For every place shifted right, the number is halved.

Forget manual gears mate. Everyone drives binary shift these days.

4) If a number is shifted 3 places right, it would be halved three times (i.e. divided by $2^3 = 8$).
If a number were shifted 4 places left, it would be doubled four times (i.e. multiplied by $2^4 = 16$).

5) If you're only working with 8-bit numbers, binary shifts can cause 1s to 'drop off' the end.
Losing 1s in a left shift will give a very different answer to the multiplication (see below).
Losing 1s in a right shift will give an inaccurate answer (rounded down to the nearest whole number).

Examples of Binary Shifts

EXAMPLE: Perform a 3 place left shift on the 8-bit binary number 00101001.
Explain the effect this will have on the number and problems that may occur.

| 0 | 0 | 1 | 0 | 1 | 0 | 0 | 1 |

1) Write down the original binary number, then shift all digits 3 places to the left.

| 0 | 0 | 1 | 0 | 1 | 0 | 0 | 1 | 0 | 0 | 0 |

2) Fill in the gaps on the right with 0s.
The number has been doubled three times, so it has been multiplied by $2^3 = 8$.

If there are only 8 bits available to store the number, then a 1 will drop off the end — this will make the answer to the calculation wrong.

In decimal, this is 41 × 8 = 328, but the 8-bit answer is 72.

EXAMPLE: Perform a 2 place right shift on the binary number 00111100.
What effect will this have on the number?

1) Write down the original binary number, then shift all digits 2 places to the right.

| 0 | 0 | 1 | 1 | 1 | 1 | 0 | 0 |

2) Fill in the gaps on the left with 0s.

| 0 | 0 | 0 | 0 | 1 | 1 | 1 | 1 | X | X |

A 2 place right shift gives the binary number 00001111.
As this is a 2 place shift, the original number will have been halved twice (so divided by $2^2 = 4$).

Dividing using a right binary shift has the same effect as using the DIV operator (p9) — your answer would not take into account any remainders.

It's just a shift to the left (and then a shift to the riiiiiiiiiiiiiiiiiiiiiight)...

Binary shifts are really good for doing super fast multiplication and division, but only by powers of 2.
If you're losing 1s on a right shift, your answer will be inaccurate (and on a left shift, it'll be way out).

Hexadecimal Numbers

Hexadecimal (hex) is another number system used regularly in programming.
Hex uses a combination of numerals and letters in order to represent a number.

Hexadecimal numbers are Shorter than Binary

1) Hexadecimal (or base-16) uses sixteen different digits.

2) A single hex digit can represent any decimal number from 0-15. To represent 0-15 in binary would require 4 bits (a nibble), so each hex digit equates to a nibble in binary.

3) The table shows the decimal and binary value of each hex digit.

4) Programmers often prefer hex when coding, because:

- It's simpler to remember large numbers in hex — they're far shorter than binary numbers.
- Due to hex numbers being shorter, there's less chance of input errors.
- It's easier to convert between binary and hex than binary and decimal.

Decimal	Hex	Binary	Decimal	Hex	Binary
0	0	0000	8	8	1000
1	1	0001	9	9	1001
2	2	0010	10	A	1010
3	3	0011	11	B	1011
4	4	0100	12	C	1100
5	5	0101	13	D	1101
6	6	0110	14	E	1110
7	7	0111	15	F	1111

Computers themselves do not use hex — they still have to convert everything to binary to process it.

Convert Hex to Decimal by Multiplying each Digit

In hex, moving right to left, place values increase in powers of 16.

4096	256	16	1

To convert from hex to decimal, draw up a table, fill in the boxes, then multiply — just like in this example:

EXAMPLES:

1. Convert the hexadecimal number 87 into decimal.

Luckily in the exam you'll only have to convert two digit hex numbers like in these examples.

1) First, draw this table, then write in your hex number.

16	1
8	7

2) Multiply the numbers in each column.

$8 \times 16 = 128$ $7 \times 1 = 7$

3) Add up the results: $128 + 7 = 135$ So the hex number 87 is 135 in decimal.

To convert from decimal to hex, draw the table but use division to fill it in.

Remember, hex goes from 0-9, then A to F.

2. Convert the decimal number 106 into hexadecimal.

1) Start at the left. Divide 106 by 16, then hold onto the remainder.
$106 \div 16 = 6 \text{ r } 10$

16	1
6	A

2) Divide the remainder from the last calculation by 1.
$10 \div 1 = 10 = A$

So the decimal number 106 is 6A in hexadecimal.

Hex can be a blessing and a curse...

Sometimes, hex and decimal can look fairly similar (as they both contain 0-9), so make sure you've got them the right way round when converting — 65 in hexadecimal is NOT the same as 65 in decimal. Learn the hex table and its advantages, then cover it all up and write everything you can remember.

Hexadecimal Numbers

Convert Binary to Hex by splitting it into Nibbles

1) Each hex digit is equal to a <u>nibble</u> in binary, so it is possible to convert from binary to hex by splitting the binary code into <u>4-bit chunks</u>.

2) Binary to hex conversions can be much <u>easier</u> than converting from binary to decimal, as you only have to deal with the nibbles <u>one at a time</u>.

Paul always eats food in 4-bit chunks. Get on with it, Paul.

EXAMPLE: Convert the binary number 10111001 to hexadecimal.

Remember, hex only uses letters for decimal values between 10-15.

1) Firstly, <u>split</u> the binary number into <u>nibbles</u>: 1011 1001

2) Draw a table with columns labelled 1, 2, 4, 8, then <u>repeat</u> the values for as many nibbles as you require.

3) Fill in the table with your binary number.

4) For <u>each nibble</u>, add up the numbers with a 1 in the column, then convert this value to hex.

5) Put the hex values <u>together</u>, and voila — you're done.

8	4	2	1	8	4	2	1
1	O	1	1	1	O	O	1

$8 + 2 + 1 = 11$
$= \underline{B}$

$8 + 1 = \underline{9}$

The binary number 10111001 is B9 in hexadecimal.

If the binary number can't be split into nibbles, you'll have to stick some zeros on the front.

EXAMPLE: Convert the binary number 111110 to hexadecimal.

1) Add <u>zeros</u> to the <u>front</u> of the binary number, so that you can split it into nibbles. ⟶ 0011 1110

2) Draw a repeating table of 1, 2, 4 and 8, as above.

3) Write your binary number in the table.

4) Add up <u>each nibble</u> and <u>convert</u> each value to <u>hex</u>.

5) Put the hex values together.

8	4	2	1	8	4	2	1
O	O	1	1	1	1	1	O

$2 + 1 = \underline{3}$

$8 + 4 + 2 = 14$
$= \underline{E}$

The binary number 111110 is 3E in hexadecimal.

For Hex to Binary, use each Digit's Decimal Value

To convert the <u>opposite</u> way (from <u>hex</u> to <u>binary</u>) convert each hex digit into binary, then just put the binary numbers together.

EXAMPLE: Convert the hexadecimal number 8C to binary.

1) First, find the decimal value of each digit: 8 = 8 in decimal   C = 12 in decimal

2) Find the binary value of each decimal number:

8	4	2	1
1	O	O	O

8 = 1000 in binary

8	4	2	1
1	1	O	O

12 = 1100 in binary

3) Put the nibbles together to get the equivalent binary number.

The hexadecimal number 8C is 10001100 in binary.

This page has so many nibbles it could spoil your lunch...

The key with converting binary to hexadecimal is to split the binary up into chunks of 4 bits, each with columns labelled 1, 2, 4 and 8. Then work out the individual hex values and put them together.

Characters

Almost everything can be represented as binary code — words, images and sound can all be turned into bits and processed by a computer. Firstly let's look at words, which are made up of different characters.

Binary can be used to represent Characters

1) Alphanumeric characters are used to make words and strings (see p11). They include uppercase and lowercase letters, the digits 0-9, and symbols like ? + and £.

2) Computers are unable to process these characters directly as they only process binary code. So they need a way of converting these characters to binary code and vice versa. They can do this using character sets.

> Character sets are collections of characters that a computer recognises from their binary representation.

Don't mistake a character set for a font. A character set is what determines the letter — the font you use just displays that letter in a certain way.

3) As well as the alphanumeric characters mentioned above, character sets also contain special characters which do certain commands (e.g. space, enter and delete).

4) So when you press a button on your keyboard it sends a binary signal to the computer telling it which key you pressed. The computer then uses the character set's encoding to translate the binary code into a particular character.

The number of Bits you'll need is based on the Character Set

Different character sets can have different amounts of characters. The number of characters in a character set determines how many bits you'll need for the character set's encoding.

- **7-bit ASCII** is a character set used to represent characters in the English language. Each ASCII character is given a 7-bit binary code — this means it can represent a total of 128 different characters, including all the letters in the English alphabet, numbers, symbols and commands.

- An extra bit (usually 0) is sometimes added to the start of the binary code for each ASCII character so that it fits nicely into 1 byte.

- The codes for numbers, uppercase letters and lowercase letters are ordered (A comes before B comes before C...) with symbols and commands scattered around.
E.g. From the table, the code for B is 66 in decimal. The code for E would be 3 after B, which is 66 + 3 = 69 in decimal or 1000101 in binary.

Character	Binary	Hex	Decimal
Backspace	0001000	8	8
O	0110000	30	48
1	0110001	31	49
=	0111101	3D	61
A	1000001	41	65
B	1000010	42	66
]	1011101	5D	93
a	1100001	61	97
b	1100010	62	98

Some examples of ASCII characters.

Extended ASCII uses 8-bit binary codes to represent 256 characters. The first 128 are the same as 7-bit ASCII but with a O in front. The others are used for things like maths symbols, and characters from other languages like French and German.

- **Unicode®** comes in several different forms and tries to cover every possible letter or symbol that might be written. Unlike ASCII, Unicode® uses multiple bytes for each character.

- The best thing about Unicode® is that it covers all major languages, even those that use a completely different alphabet like Greek, Russian and Chinese.

- The first 128 codes in Unicode® are the same as ASCII.

00010010 01101111
10110101 10011010

My computer started typing in Greek — it was out of character...

You don't need to remember the ASCII codes for any specific characters, but if you're given the ASCII code of one character (e.g. T) you should be able to work out the ASCII code for another character (e.g. W).

Storing Images

Images and sounds are pieces of data stored on computers — so, naturally, they're made of bits (p37). How those bits turn into your latest selfie or your favourite Jason-B song is covered on the next two pages.

Images *are stored as a series of Pixels*

1) The type of image you use most often is a <u>bitmap</u> — they're mainly used for photos. Bitmap images are made up of lots of tiny dots, called <u>pixels</u> (short for picture elements).

2) The <u>colour</u> of each pixel is represented by a <u>binary</u> code. The number of colours available in an image is related to the number of <u>bits</u> the code has.

3) <u>Black-and-white</u> images only use two colours, so they only need <u>1-bit</u> to represent each pixel — <u>0 for white</u> and <u>1 for black</u>.

4) <u>2-bit images</u> can be made up of four colours. Each pixel can be one of four binary values — <u>00, 01, 10</u> and <u>11</u>.

5) You can make a <u>greater range</u> of shades and colours by <u>increasing the number of bits</u> for each pixel.

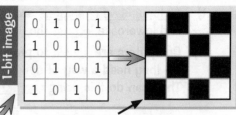

This image would have the bit pattern 0101 1010 0101 1010

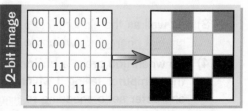

Computer screens are often divided into <u>millions of pixels</u> arranged in rows and columns.

Increasing Colour Depth and Image Size increases the File Size

1) The <u>colour depth</u> is the <u>number of bits</u> used for <u>each pixel</u>.

2) Given the colour depth you can work out <u>how many colours</u> can be made using this <u>formula</u>:

> **Total number of colours = 2^n (where n = number of bits per pixel, or bpp)**

> **1-bit image: 2^1 = 2 colours**   **4-bit image: 2^4 = 16 colours**   **24-bit image: 2^{24} = 16 777 216 colours**

3) Most devices use a <u>24-bit colour depth</u>, with 8 bits used to indicate the levels of <u>red</u>, <u>green</u> and <u>blue</u> needed for each pixel. It's estimated that the human eye can see around 10 million different colours, so a 24-bit colour depth should cover every colour that you could possibly see.

4) The <u>image size</u> is the <u>number of pixels</u> in the image. It's usually given as <u>width × height</u>. The <u>more pixels</u> the image is made of, the <u>better the quality</u> of the image. E.g. if an image has an image size of 1200 × 800, it means that it is made up of 960 000 pixels. If the size was decreased to 600 × 400, it would only have 240 000 pixels, so would have a lower quality.

5) To work out <u>how many bits</u> an image will take up, use the <u>formula</u>:

> **File size (in bits) = image size × colour depth = width × height × colour depth**

6) Using a <u>larger</u> image size or colour depth means that there are <u>more bits</u> in the image. This can give a <u>higher-quality image</u>, but also increases the <u>file size</u>.

EXAMPLE: Calculate the file size, in MB, of an 8-bit image that is 2000 pixels wide and 1000 pixels high.

1) First, use the <u>formula</u> to find the <u>size in bits</u>:   2000 × 1000 × 8 = 16 000 000 bits

2) <u>Divide by 8</u> to convert to <u>bytes</u>:   16 000 000 ÷ 8 = 2 000 000 bytes

3) Finally, <u>divide by 1000 twice</u> to convert to <u>MB</u>:   2 000 000 ÷ 1000 ÷ 1000 = 2 MB

Mariana blue — the colour with the greatest depth...

Bet you didn't know images had so much going on. Remember that these types of images are called bitmaps — they're the ones made out of pixels. There is also another type called a vector image — vectors are made of simple shapes, all different blocks of colour. We tend to use them for computer-made graphics, like this picture of a distinguished goat that's wandered onto this tip.

Storing Sound

Like images, sound is made up of bits and stored in files on a computer. Or rather, digital sound is — the other type of sound, analogue, doesn't get on well with computers very much, so we've got to turn it into digital first.

Sound is Sampled and stored Digitally

1) Sound is recorded by a microphone as an <u>analogue</u> signal. Analogue signals are pieces of <u>continually changing</u> data.

2) Analogue signals need to be converted into <u>digital</u> data so that computers can read and store sound files. This is done by <u>analogue to digital converters</u>, which are found in most modern recording devices.

> Oooooh yeah, I wanna sample your amplituuuuude...

3) The process of converting analogue to digital is called <u>sampling</u>:

The orange line shows the analogue sound wave — it's one <u>continuous</u> piece of data which <u>keeps changing</u>.

To convert the analogue recording to digital data, we <u>sample</u> the <u>amplitude</u> of the wave at <u>regular intervals</u> (shown by the blue dots on the graph). The amplitude can only take certain values depending on the <u>sample resolution</u> (see below). Once the device has sampled the recording, it creates the curve <u>digitally</u> like this.

Each block of data matches where each sample was taken.

The digital data is about the same shape as the analogue wave, but it's <u>not continuous</u>. It's <u>lost</u> a lot of data — e.g. the last peak in the analogue wave is much flatter in the digital data.

The digital data can be improved by taking samples <u>more regularly</u> — most music isn't sampled every second but more like several times a <u>millisecond</u>.

Several factors affect the Size and Quality of Sound Files

1) <u>Sample rate</u> (or <u>sampling frequency</u>) is how many samples you take in a second — it's measured in hertz (Hz) or kilohertz (kHz). E.g. a common sample rate is 44 100 samples per second (44 100 Hz or 44.1 kHz).

2) <u>Sample resolution</u> is the number of bits available for each sample.

> Sample rate × sample resolution is called the <u>bit rate</u>.

3) You can calculate the <u>size</u> of a sound file using this <u>formula</u>:

> **File size (in bits) = Sample rate (in Hz) × sample resolution × length (in seconds)**

4) For example, if you were to sample <u>30 seconds</u> of audio with a sample resolution of <u>8 bits</u> and a sample rate of <u>500 Hz</u>, your file would be 500 × 8 × 30 = 120 000 bits.

5) <u>Increasing</u> the sample rate means the analogue recording is sampled more often. The sampled sound will be <u>better quality</u> and will more <u>closely match</u> the original recording.

6) <u>Increasing</u> the sample resolution means the digital file picks up <u>quieter sounds</u>, even if they're happening at the same time as louder ones. This will also result in a sampled sound that is closer to the <u>quality</u> of the original recording.

7) However, increasing the sample rate or sample resolution will <u>increase the file size</u>.

Anna Log talks continuously, while Digit Al just speaks in bits...

Make sure you don't mix up sample rate and sample resolution. Sample resolution is basically the sound equivalent of colour depth in images — it's the number of bits used for each 'piece' of data in the file.

Compression

In the modern world, we're practically swimming in badly lit photos and subpar pop songs — so many, in fact, that you'd start to wonder how we can possibly store them all. The answer is down to data compression.

Sometimes we need to Compress files

1) Data compression is when we make file sizes smaller, while trying to make the compressed file as true to the original as possible.

2) Compressing data files has many uses:

- Smaller files take up less storage space on a device.
- Streaming and downloading files from the Internet is quicker as they take up less bandwidth.
- It allows web pages to load more quickly in web browsers.
- Email services normally have restrictions on the size of the attachment you can send — compressing the file allows you to send the same content with a much smaller file size.

There are Two Types of compression — Lossy and Lossless

1) Lossy compression works by permanently removing data from the file — this limits the number of bits the file needs and so reduces its size.

2) Lossless compression makes the file smaller by temporarily removing data to store the file and then restores it to its original state when it's opened.

	Pros	Cons	E.g. of File Types
Lossy	• Greatly reduced file size, meaning more files can be stored. • Lossy files take up less bandwidth so can be downloaded and streamed more quickly. • Commonly used — lots of software can read lossy files.	• Lossy compression loses data — the file can't be turned back into the original. • Lossy compression can't be used on text or software files as these files need to retain all the information of the original. • Lossy files are worse quality than the original. But, this loss in quality is normally unnoticeable.	• MP3 (audio) • AAC (audio) • JPEG (image)
Lossless	• Data is only removed temporarily so there is no reduction in quality — the compressed file should look or sound like the original. • Lossless files can be decompressed — turned back into the original. • Lossless compression can be used on text and software files.	• Only a slight reduction in file size, so lossless files still take up quite a bit of space on your device. E.g. a lossless song may have a file size of around 30 MB, while the same song with lossy compression may be 5 MB.	• FLAC (audio) • TIFF (image) • PNG (image)

 EXAMPLE: Phil has just heard a new band on the radio. He wants to download fifty of their songs from the Internet and store them on his smartphone to take on holiday. State which type of compression would be most appropriate in this situation and explain why.

Lossy compression would be the most appropriate. Lossy files are smaller so they would take up less bandwidth, meaning Phil could download the songs more quickly. Their smaller file size would also allow him to store them all on his smartphone without taking up too much storage space.

The best compression type? I'm afraid I'm at a loss...

Lossy files aren't as high quality as the originals, but the difference is normally unnoticeable to us unperceptive humans. This helps to explain why lossy file formats like JPEG (for photos) and MP3 (for music) are so popular — they save a lot of storage space and their inferior quality is hardly noticeable.

Run-Length Encoding

So compression is important when saving and transmitting data — but the real question is, how do you do it? Run-Length Encoding (RLE) is one of the two compression techniques that you should know (just run with it...)

Run-Length Encoding looks for Repeating Data

1) Run-Length Encoding (or RLE for short) is a form of lossless compression (see previous page). This means that the process reduces a file's size without losing any data.

2) It looks for consecutive repeating data in a file — called a run. Instead of storing each piece of repeated data separately, it just stores the number of times it repeats, and one copy of the data.

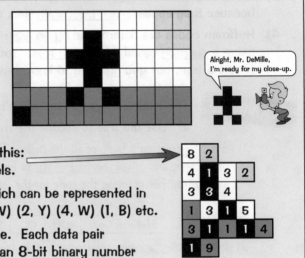

- Take a look at the bitmap image on the right.

- If the image used an 8-bit colour depth then, using the formula on p44, it would be made up of 10 × 6 × 8 = 480 bits. This can be reduced by using RLE.

- First, count the number of times the same data is repeated in each run, and store this instead.

- So this image could be compressed to look like this: E.g. the top row has 8 white, then 2 yellow pixels.

- You can store this information as data pairs, which can be represented in the format (number of pixels, colour), e.g. (8, W) (2, Y) (4, W) (1, B) etc.

- In this example, we'd have 20 data pairs to store. Each data pair consists of a number, which could be stored as an 8-bit binary number (see p38), and an 8-bit colour — so 16 bits total.

- The final compressed image would be 20 × 16 = 320 bits, rather than the 480 bits that we started with — that's a 33% decrease in file size.

Alright, Mr. DeMille, I'm ready for my close-up.

3) Run-length encoding is pretty easy to understand, but it's not perfect. If the data doesn't have many runs of repeated data, then the file size will not be significantly decreased.

You can also use RLE to compress Different Types of Data

1) Run-length encoding can also be applied to text. For example, say we have the string 'wwwwwhtttt'. In 7-bit ASCII, this would use 7 bits for each character, so 10 × 7 = 70 bits altogether.

2) 'w' occurs 5 times, then 'h' once and 't' four times. As data pairs this would be: (5, w) (1, h) (4, t). If 1 byte was used for each number, then each data pair could be stored in 8 + 7 = 15 bits. Then the encoded text would need a total of 3 × 15 = 45 bits, rather than 70.

3) You can also use RLE to encode binary data. But be warned — because 1s and 0s just take up 1 bit each, you need very long runs of repeated data for it to actually reduce the size.

EXAMPLE: Use run-length encoding to compress the following bit pattern:

00000000   01111111   11111111   11000000   00000000

Count the number of bits in each run and write down the data pairs.

Nine 0s, then seventeen 1s and fourteen 0s. So the data pairs are (9, 0) (17, 1) (14, 0).

Each data pair could be 8 bits with 7 bits for the run lengths, and 1 bit for the actual data:

00010010   00100011   00011100

9 written in binary   17 written in binary   14 written in binary

Me on a rollercoaster: (1, W), (24, O), (1, !)...

Learning the content above will really help you understand how text, images and sound can be compressed without losing any data. Just remember that run-length encoding doesn't always reduce the size of a file — like buying new expensive trainers, you need long runs to make it worthwhile.

Huffman Coding

Another <u>lossless</u> compression technique that you'll need to know is Huffman coding. Enjoy. It's a good'un.

Huffman Coding uses the Frequency of each data value

1) Each <u>data value</u> in a <u>file</u> (e.g. a character in a text file) often takes up the <u>same amount of space</u>. For example, text encoded in 7-bit ASCII (see p43) uses 7 bits per character, but this can be <u>inefficient</u>.

2) <u>Huffman coding</u> gives <u>each data value</u> a <u>unique binary code</u> but the codes <u>vary in length</u>. It gives <u>shorter binary codes</u> to data values that appear <u>more frequently</u>.

3) For example, in the <u>table</u> on the right, 'r', 'e' and 'a' have <u>short binary codes</u>, because they appear <u>more frequently</u> than other characters in the file.

4) Huffman codes are determined by an <u>algorithm</u> and can be represented using a <u>diagram</u> called a <u>Huffman tree</u>. You <u>don't</u> need to know how to <u>create</u> a tree, but you <u>do</u> need to know how to <u>read</u> one.

Character	Huffman Code
'r'	00
'e'	10
'a'	11
's'	010
space	0110

EXAMPLE: The Huffman tree for the string 'he sells seashells' is shown on the right.

a) Use this tree to encode the string 'he sells seashells'.

1) Start by creating a <u>table</u> of all the codes. To find a code, start from the <u>top</u> of the tree, and <u>follow the path down</u> to each letter, writing down each 0 or 1 as you go. For example, the code for the letter 'a' will be 1010.

Character	'h'	'e'	space	's'	'l'	'a'
Huffman Code	1011	00	100	11	01	1010

2) Now, just <u>replace</u> every character in the string with its <u>Huffman code</u>:

'he sells seashells' would be encoded as

1011|00|100|11|00|01|01|11|100|11|00|1010|11|1011|00|01|01|11

> If the branches aren't labelled, you might have to use a given code to figure out which direction is 0 and which is 1.

5) You can also <u>decode</u> data, using either the <u>Huffman tree</u> or a <u>table of Huffman codes</u>.

b) Decode this bit pattern, using the Huffman coding from part a):
11101100010111100101110101111010010000000111

1) Starting on the left, find the <u>first code</u> — 1 isn't a code, but 11 is the code for 's'. <u>Draw a line</u> after 11, and write an 's'.

11|1011|00|01|01|11|100|1011|1010|11|11|01|00|100|00|000|111
s h   e l l s .   h   a   s s l e .   e e   s

2) Keep going until it's <u>completely decoded</u>. So the decoded string is shells hassle eels.

You can Calculate the Number of Bits Saved

A question might ask you to <u>compare</u> the <u>number of bits needed</u> to store some data using <u>different encoding methods</u>.

c) Calculate how many bits are saved using this Huffman coding over ASCII to store the string 'he sells seashells'.

1) The string has <u>18 characters</u> (including spaces) and each character in ASCII would require <u>7 bits</u> (see p43), so: ASCII: 18 × 7 = 126 bits

2) Next, <u>count</u> the <u>number of digits</u> in the answer to part a):   Huffman coding: 44 bits

3) Finally, calculate the number of <u>bits saved</u>:   126 − 44 = 82 bits

> Another option might be to use a fixed-length encoding. This would require at least 3 bits per character (3 bits can encode up to 2^3 = 8 different characters), so the string would need 18 × 3 = 54 bits.

Don't go off in a huff man, it's only a type of compression...

Huffman coding is a really handy compression technique — plus, Huffman trees look particularly splendid in Autumn. You should know how to both encode and decode data using a Huffman tree.

Revision Questions for Section Four

Section Four is done and dusted, so all you've got to do now is try these questions, then put your feet up.

• Try these questions and <u>tick off each one</u> when you <u>get it right</u>.

• When you've done <u>all the questions</u> for a topic and are <u>completely happy</u> with it, tick off the topic.

Logic and Units (p34-37) ☑

1) For each of the 4 main logic gates: a) Draw its symbol.
   b) State how many inputs and outputs it has.
   c) Draw its truth table. ☑

2)* Write a Boolean expression (in words and in symbols) and draw the truth table for the logic diagram on the right. ☑

Input A ──┐
Input B ──┤)──┐
Input C ──────┤)── Output

3) Why is binary used by computers? ☑

4) Put these units in order of size: Terabyte, Byte, Kilobyte, Gigabyte, Megabyte ☑

5)* A hard drive has a storage capacity of 200 megabytes.
   a) How many gigabytes is this?   b) How many bits is this? ☑

Binary and Hexadecimal (p38-42) ☑

6)* Add the binary numbers 01011101 and 00110010. ☑

7) What effect do left and right shifts have on binary numbers? ☑

8)* Convert the following decimal numbers to: a) binary   b) hexadecimal
   (i) 17   (ii) 148   (iii) 240 ☑

9)* Convert the following binary numbers to: a) decimal   b) hexadecimal
   (i) 00111000   (ii) 10011111   (iii) 101011 ☑

10)* Convert these hexadecimal numbers to: a) decimal   b) binary
    (i) 4A   (ii) 75   (iii) D9 ☑

11) Give three reasons why programmers prefer hexadecimal over binary and decimal. ☑

Characters, Images and Sound (p43-45) ☑

12) What is the definition of a character set? ☑

13) Give the four types of characters that are included in a character set. ☑

14) What are the two main character sets? Give a feature of each. ☑

15) Define the following terms: a) pixel   b) bitmap   c) colour depth   d) image size ☑

16) Give two effects of choosing a greater image size or colour depth for an image. ☑

17) In no more than four bullet points, explain how audio sampling works. ☑

18) Give a definition for each of the following and explain what happens when you increase each of them:
    a) sample rate   b) sample resolution ☑

Compression and Coding (p46-48) ☑

19) Give four reasons why you might want to compress data. ☑

20) What is the difference between lossy compression and lossless compression? ☑

21) Give three reasons why you might want to use: a) lossy compression   b) lossless compression ☑

22)* The file letters.txt contains the string 'PPPPQQRRRSSSSSSPPPPPQQQ'.
    a) Encode this string using run-length encoding.
    b) Use the tree on the right to create a table of Huffman codes for this string.
    c) Calculate the number of bits needed to store the string if it was encoded with:
       (i) 7-bit ASCII   (ii) Huffman coding
       (iii) Run-length encoding (if each data pair used 2 bytes). ☑

```
      0 ╱ ╲ 1
     P    ●
        0 ╱ ╲ 1
       S    ●
          0 ╱ ╲ 1
         R    Q
```

*Answers on p81

Computer Systems

Now it's time to take a step back and ask yourself the most important question — what even is a computer?

A Computer is a Machine that Processes Data

1) The purpose of a computer is to take <u>data</u>, <u>process</u> it, then <u>output</u> it.
   Computers were created to help process data and complete tasks <u>more efficiently</u> than humans.

2) A <u>computer system</u> consists of <u>hardware</u> and <u>software</u> that work together to process data / complete tasks.

   - Hardware is the <u>physical</u> stuff that makes up your computer system, like the CPU, motherboard, monitor and printer.

     External pieces of hardware like the keyboard, mouse and printer are called <u>peripherals</u>.

   - Software is the <u>programs</u> that a computer system runs. You can have <u>application software</u> (programs that help the user perform specific tasks, e.g. word processors, web browsers, database software, games, etc.) and <u>system software</u> (operating systems, utilities, etc. — see p57-59).

3) There are <u>many types</u> of computer system. These range from small devices like calculators and watches, up to large <u>supercomputers</u> used by banks or for scientific applications. Computers may be <u>general purpose</u> (designed to perform <u>many tasks</u>, e.g. PCs and tablets) or <u>dedicated systems</u> (designed for <u>one particular</u> function, e.g. controlling traffic lights or an aeroplane).

Embedded Systems are Computers inside a Larger System

1) <u>Embedded systems</u> are computers <u>built into other devices</u>, like dishwashers, microwaves and TVs. They are usually dedicated systems.

2) Embedded systems are often used as <u>control systems</u> — they <u>monitor</u> and <u>control</u> machinery in order to achieve a desired result. E.g. In a <u>dishwasher</u> the embedded system could control the water pumps and water release mechanisms, manage the various dishwasher cycles and control the thermostat to keep the water at an appropriate temperature.

3) As they're <u>dedicated</u> to a single task, embedded systems are usually easier to <u>design</u>, cheaper to <u>produce</u>, and more <u>efficient</u> at doing their task than a general purpose computer.

Computers contain Components which Work Together

This section covers the main hardware components of a computer.
As a <u>genuinely fun</u> warm-up, let's take a look inside a typical desktop PC.

<u>Power supply</u> — supplies power to motherboard, optical and hard drives, and other hardware.

<u>Case cooling fan</u> — extracts hot air from the computer case.

<u>CPU heat sink and cooling fan</u> — keeps the CPU at a steady temperature (CPUs generate a lot of heat).

<u>CPU</u> (hidden under the heat sink) — the most important component. Does all the processing. See p51-52.

<u>Optical drive</u> — for read/writing of optical discs. See p56.

<u>Ghost</u> in the machine.

<u>RAM sticks</u> (computer memory) slot in here. See p53-54.

<u>Hard Disk Drive</u> — Internal secondary storage. See p55.

The <u>graphics card</u> slots in here. See p54.

<u>Motherboard</u> — The main circuit board in the computer, where the hardware is connected.

Hardware — clothes that make you look dead tough, innit...

Make sure you know all of these components before moving on — they'll crop up a lot in this section...

The CPU

The CPU is mega-important — it's the main component of a computer, so here are two whole pages about it. Yay.

The CPU is the Central Processing Unit

1) The CPU is the brain of the computer system.

2) It processes all of the data and instructions that make the system work.

3) The processing power of a CPU depends on different characteristics, like its clock speed, number of cores and cache size and type — see p54.

4) The CPU architecture describes the main components of the CPU, how they interact with each other, and with other parts of the computer system. Von Neumann and Harvard are the two main types of architecture. You will need to know about Von Neumann — see next page.

CPUs contain 100s of gold pins — some of these transmit data, others supply power to the CPU. (Aside: CPUs are shiny and pretty)

The CPU has Five Main Parts

The Control Unit (CU)

- The control unit is in overall control of the CPU. Its main job is to manage the fetching, decoding and execution of program instructions by following the Fetch-Execute cycle (see next page).
- It controls the flow of data inside the CPU (to registers, ALU, cache — see below) and outside the CPU (to main memory and input/output devices).

The Arithmetic Logic Unit (ALU)

- The ALU basically does all the calculations.
- It completes simple addition and subtraction, compares the size of numbers and can do multiplications and divisions using repeated addition and subtraction.
- It performs logic operations such as AND, OR and NOT (p34) and binary shifts (p40) — remember, computers process binary data.
- Registers (see below) are used to store intermediate results of calculations.

3 PLUS 2 IS 5! TRUE OR FALSE IS TRUE!

Cache

- Cache is very fast memory in the CPU. It's slower than the registers (see below), but faster than RAM (p53).
- It stores regularly used data so that the CPU can access it quickly the next time it's needed. When the CPU requests data, it checks its cache first to see if the data is there. If not, it will fetch it from RAM.
- Caches have a very low capacity and are expensive compared to RAM and secondary storage.

The Clock

- The clock sends out a signal that continually cycles between 1 and 0, usually at a constant rate.
- The signal is used to synchronise when instructions will be carried out (like a metronome).
- The number of clock cycles (or clock ticks) per second is called the clock speed (p54).

Buses

- Buses are collections of wires that are used to transmit data between components of the CPU, and to other parts of the computer system.
- A processor may have separate buses for carrying data, instructions and memory addresses.

The CPU also contains various registers which temporarily hold tiny bits of data needed by the CPU. They are super-quick to read/write to, way quicker than any other form of memory.

What's a CPU's favourite outdoor activity? Geocaching...

It's important that you know all about the different components of a CPU. Try learning everything you can about each one, then cover up the page and write down as many notes as you can.

The CPU

Now let's look at the Von Neumann architecture and what the CPU does in a bit more detail.
Von Neumann came up with his design in 1945 and it still describes how most computers work today.

Von Neumann's Design Revolutionised Computing

The Von Neumann architecture describes a system where the CPU runs programs stored in memory.
Programs consist of instructions and data which are stored in memory addresses.

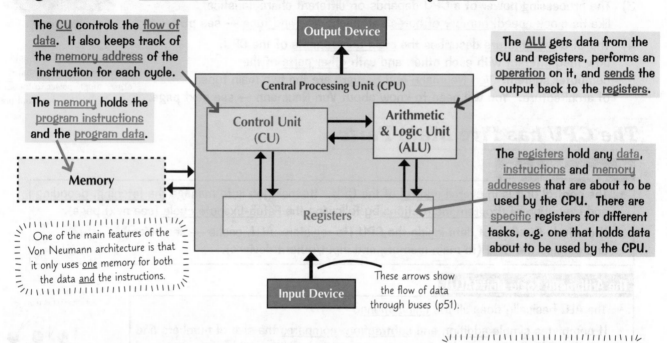

The CU controls the flow of data. It also keeps track of the memory address of the instruction for each cycle.

The memory holds the program instructions and the program data.

Memory

One of the main features of the Von Neumann architecture is that it only uses one memory for both the data and the instructions.

Output Device

Central Processing Unit (CPU)

Control Unit (CU)

Arithmetic & Logic Unit (ALU)

Registers

Input Device

The ALU gets data from the CU and registers, performs an operation on it, and sends the output back to the registers.

The registers hold any data, instructions and memory addresses that are about to be used by the CPU. There are specific registers for different tasks, e.g. one that holds data about to be used by the CPU.

These arrows show the flow of data through buses (p51).

CPUs follow the Fetch-Execute Cycle

Each Fetch-Execute cycle will take multiple clock cycles (see previous page).

Essentially, all a CPU does is carry out instructions, one after another, billions of times a second.
The Fetch-Execute cycle (also called the Fetch-Decode-Execute cycle) describes how it does it.

FETCH INSTRUCTION

1) The control unit reads the memory address of the next CPU instruction.
2) The instruction stored in that address is copied from memory to one of the registers.
3) The memory address in the control unit is incremented to point to the address of the next instruction, ready for the next cycle.

DECODE INSTRUCTION

1) The instruction that was copied from memory is decoded by the control unit.
2) The control unit prepares for the next step, e.g. by loading other values into the registers.

EXECUTE INSTRUCTION

The instruction is performed. This could be: load data from memory, write data to memory, do a calculation or logic operation (using the ALU), change the address in the CU, or halt the program.

Well, now I know why my computer goes through so many dogs...

I won't lie to you, this page is tougher than a really tough piece of toffee. Just keep going through the cycle until it sticks — it uses the memory address to fetch the instruction, it decodes the instruction and gets everything ready for execution, and then it actually carries the instruction out. The parts of the CPU are important as well — remember, the ALU does the calculations, the registers hold data and instructions waiting to be used, and the CU tells everything else what to do.

Memory

As you'll have gathered from the last page, memory is a pretty fundamental part of a computer. It stores all the instructions that the CPU follows. Without memory, a computer wouldn't know what to do with itself.

There are Four Different Types of Memory

1) Registers — see page 52
2) Random Access Memory (RAM) — see below
3) Cache — see page 51
4) Read Only Memory (ROM) — see below

RAM is High Speed, Volatile memory

1) RAM (or Random Access Memory) is used as main memory in a computer. It can be read and written to. RAM is volatile.

> • Volatile memory is temporary memory. It requires power to retain its data.
> • Non-volatile memory is permanent memory — it keeps its contents even when it has no power.

2) RAM is where all data, files and programs are stored while they're being used.
3) When a computer boots up, the operating system is copied from secondary storage to RAM.
4) When software applications, documents and files are opened, they are copied from secondary storage to RAM. They stay in RAM until the files or applications are closed.
5) RAM is slower than CPU cache memory, but way faster than secondary storage. *Secondary storage is covered on p55-56.*

That's RAM covered, which can mean only ROM thing...

ROM tells the CPU how to Boot Up

1) ROM ('Read Only Memory') is also used as main memory, but is non-volatile. As it says on the tin, it can only be read, not written to.
2) ROM comes on a small, factory-made chip built into the motherboard. *The BIOS is a type of firmware — hardware-specific software built in to a device. Embedded systems (p50) are controlled by firmware.*
3) It contains all the instructions a computer needs to properly boot up. These instructions are called the BIOS (Basic Input Output System).
4) As soon as the computer is powered on, the CPU reads the instructions from ROM. This tells the CPU to perform self checks and set up the computer, e.g. test the memory is working OK, see what hardware is present and copy the operating system into RAM.
5) Although the CPU can only read ROM, it is possible to update ('flash') the BIOS on a ROM chip.

Systems have Different RAM/ROM Requirements

The amount of RAM and ROM that a system needs depends on the purpose and type of the system.

Non-embedded systems	Embedded systems
• Non-embedded systems usually have much more RAM than ROM because they often need to write data to main memory.	• Embedded systems usually have more ROM than RAM because they don't write much (if any) data to memory.
• ROM is typically only used for BIOS, which doesn't require much memory.	• They don't tend to have secondary storage (p55-56) so ROM is used to store all programs.
• ROM and RAM are usually stored on the motherboard, away from the CPU.	• ROM and RAM are often stored on the same chip as the CPU to reduce physical space needed and cost.

Woah, woah, back off — this memory's volatile...

The memory (RAM) is where the computer puts everything it's working on. Don't confuse memory with secondary storage — e.g. if a computer has a 2 TB (see p37) hard drive, never say it has 2 TB of memory.

CPU and System Performance

All sorts of things affect the speed of a computer system, but the biggest factors are usually to do with the hardware. Choice of CPU, RAM and GPU (see below) can all have big effects on performance.

CPU Performance depends on Clock Speed, Cores and Cache

Clock speed

- For most desktop computers, <u>clock speed</u> (see p51) is somewhere around 3.5 GHz (i.e. 3.5 billion clock cycles per second). This determines the <u>number of instructions</u> a single processor core can carry out per <u>second</u> — the <u>higher</u> the clock speed, the <u>more</u> instructions that can be carried out per second.
- Some CPUs can be <u>overclocked</u> to make them run at a higher clock speed than the factory-set rate. But it's risky if not done properly — it can make CPUs <u>overheat</u>, causing <u>crashes</u> or permanent <u>damage</u> to the system. High performance <u>cooling systems</u> (e.g. water cooling) are usually needed.

CPU Cores

- Each <u>core</u> in a CPU can process data <u>independently</u> of the rest.
- The <u>more cores</u> a CPU has, the <u>more instructions</u> it can carry out at once, so the faster it can process a batch of data.
- Most PCs and smartphones have 4 or more cores these days.

It's <u>not</u> quite as simple as 'doubling the number of cores doubles performance'. Software needs to be <u>designed</u> to use multicore processing. And not all processing tasks can be split evenly between cores — some steps will <u>depend</u> on others, meaning one core may end up waiting for another core to catch up.

Cache

- Cache (p51) is data storage inside the CPU that's much <u>faster than RAM</u>.
- A <u>larger</u> CPU cache gives the CPU faster access to <u>more data</u> it needs to process.
- Cache <u>speed</u> is based on how <u>far</u> it is from the <u>CPU</u>.
  - Certain <u>types</u> of cache will be stored <u>on</u> the CPU itself, which mean they are <u>extremely fast</u> to access.
  - Other types are stored <u>further away</u>, e.g. on the <u>motherboard</u>, so they are <u>slightly slower</u> to access.

Generally, CPUs with <u>higher clock speeds</u>, <u>more cores</u> or <u>larger caches</u> will have better performance, but will also be more expensive.

Overall Performance is affected by Other Components too

RAM

1) If a computer has <u>too little</u> RAM, it may not be able to keep all application data loaded at once, slowing the system down.
2) The <u>more RAM</u>, the <u>more applications</u> or more <u>memory-intensive</u> applications it can smoothly run, making it faster overall.
3) If the computer <u>already</u> has plenty of RAM to run everything the user wants, increasing RAM may make <u>no</u> difference to performance.

RAM comes on sticks which plug into slots on the motherboard.

GPU

1) <u>GPUs</u> (graphics processing units) handle <u>graphics</u> and <u>image</u> processing. They relieve the <u>processing load</u> on the CPU, freeing it to do other things.
2) Computers have <u>basic</u> GPUs integrated onto the <u>motherboard</u> or the <u>CPU</u>, but you can install a <u>dedicated</u> GPU (graphics card) to improve performance in graphics-intensive applications, e.g. PC <u>gaming</u> and design software.

Cooling fan

Sheep

Video Outputs

PCI interface slots into motherboard.

A whopping-great graphics card — explains why gaming PCs are massive.

You can buy apples with 4 cores now? Don't be daft...

To be honest, there are quite a few simplifications going on here. In the real world, there's a lot more to CPU performance than cores, cache and clock speed. But this level of detail is all you need at GCSE. Using <u>SSDs</u> rather than traditional hard drives is another way to speed up a computer — see p55.

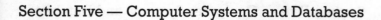

Secondary Storage

"Secondary storage!", I hear you cry. "But what about primary?" It's OK, we've just covered that, as you'll see...

There are Two Main Tiers of Storage

1) Primary storage refers to the memory areas that the CPU can access directly, like CPU registers, cache, ROM and RAM. Primary storage has the fastest read/write speeds and is mostly volatile (p53).

2) Secondary storage is non-volatile storage that isn't directly accessible by the CPU. It's where all data (applications, user files and the OS) are stored when not in use. It includes magnetic hard disk drives, solid state drives, CDs and SD cards. Read/write speeds for secondary storage are much slower compared to primary storage.

> There's also tertiary storage, which is used for long term data storage (mainly used for archives and backups of huge amounts of data).

Magnetic Hard Disks are High-Capacity, Reliable Storage

1) Hard disk drives (HDDs) are the traditional internal storage in PCs and laptops.

2) A hard disk drive is made up of a stack of magnetised metal disks spinning at a rate between 5400 and 15000 rpm (revolutions per minute).

3) Data is stored magnetically in small areas called sectors within circular tracks. Read/write heads on a moving arm are used to access sectors on the disks.

4) Portable HDDs are popular for backing up and transporting large amounts of data.

5) Despite their moving parts, HDDs are generally very long lasting and reliable, although they could be damaged by large impacts like being dropped.

Data track
Sector
Read / Write head
Movable arm

Other types of magnetic storage

- Another type of magnetic storage is magnetic tape. It has a very high capacity and an extremely low cost per GB. It's often used by large organisations for backing up large amounts of data.

- Reels of tape are stored in plastic cassettes. Tapes are read/written sequentially by the tape drive i.e. from beginning to end. This means it can be slow when finding specific data stored on them, but once it's in the right place, reading/writing to the tape is very fast.

Solid State Drives are Fast and Reliable Secondary Storage

1) Solid State Drives (SSDs) have no moving parts — they tend to use flash storage which stores data in electrical circuits by trapping electrons. Like HDDs, SSDs are typically used for internal storage.

2) SSDs have significantly faster read/write times than HDDs. Using a SSD rather than a traditional HDD can give much quicker times for booting up and opening programs and files.

3) Hybrid drives exist which use solid state storage for the OS and programs, and a hard disk for data.

4) Like HDDs, portable SSDs can be used to back up and transport data.

Other types of flash storage

- USB pen drives and memory cards (e.g. SD cards) are also flash-based, solid-state storage.

- They're much slower than SSDs and have a much shorter read/write life.

- They're used to expand the storage capacity of small devices like cameras, smartphones and tablets (which are too small for SSDs or HDDs). Their capacity is very high relative to their tiny size.

HDDs vs SSDs — Who wins, You Decide...

Advantages of HDDs	Advantages of SSDs
• HDDs are cheaper.	• SSDs are faster.
• Both are high capacity, but HDDs are higher.	• SSDs don't need defragmenting (see p59).
• HDDs have a longer read/write life than SSDs — SSDs can only be written a certain number of times before they begin to deteriorate.	• SSDs are more shock-proof than HDDs.
	• HDDs make some noise, SSDs are silent.

Section Five — Computer Systems and Databases

Secondary Storage

Be careful with your terminology. Storage <u>media</u> refers to the actual thing that holds the data, e.g. optical discs (see below). A storage <u>device</u> is the thing that reads/writes data to media, e.g. HDDs or optical drive.

Optical Discs are Cheap and Robust Secondary Storage

1) Optical discs are things like <u>CDs</u>, <u>DVDs</u> and <u>Blu-Ray</u>™ discs.

2) CDs can hold around 700 MB of data, DVDs can hold around 4.7 GB and Blu-Rays can hold around 25 GB.

3) Optical discs come in three forms:

- <u>read-only</u> (e.g. CD-ROM / DVD-ROM / BD-ROM)
- <u>write-once</u> (e.g. CD-R / DVD-R / BD-R)
- <u>rewritable</u> (e.g. CD-RW / DVD-RW / BD-RW)

Laser — Data pits — Reflective surface

Data is stored as <u>microscopic indentations</u> on the shiny surface of the disc. Data is read by shining a laser beam on the surface and detecting changes in the position of the <u>reflected beam</u>.

4) Nowadays, their use is <u>declining</u>:
- <u>Streaming</u> and <u>download</u> services have reduced the need for optical discs.
- Modern devices like <u>phones</u> and <u>tablets</u> don't have optical drives.
- DVD-Rs and DVD-RWs used to be popular for backing up data, but they can't compete with flash storage devices due to their <u>low capacity</u> per disc, very <u>slow</u> read/write speeds and poor reliability of <u>RW</u> discs.

5) They do have some <u>advantages</u> — they're very cheap (per GB), portable, and won't be damaged by <u>water</u> or <u>shocks</u> (although they are easily <u>scratched</u>).

Optical discs are still useful as mirrors. Or, bury them in flowerbeds to scare away cats.

Cloud Storage uses the Internet to store files and applications

<u>Cloud storage</u> is a service where files can be <u>uploaded</u> via the <u>Internet</u> to a <u>remote server</u> (where it is usually stored on HDDs/SSDs). You normally pay a <u>subscription</u>, though some provide a <u>limited service</u> for <u>free</u> (p75).

Pros of the cloud

- Users can access files from <u>any connected device</u>.
- Files can be <u>shared</u> with others or made <u>public</u>.
- Easy to <u>increase</u> how much <u>storage</u> is available.
- <u>No</u> need to buy <u>expensive hardware</u> to store data.
- <u>No</u> need to pay <u>IT staff</u> to manage the hardware.
- Cloud host provides <u>security</u> and <u>backups</u> for you.
- Can be <u>cheap/free</u> if <u>not much storage</u> is required.

Cons of the cloud

- Need <u>connection to the Internet</u> to access files.
- Upload/download speed depends on <u>bandwidth</u>.
- <u>Dependent on host</u> for security and backups.
- Stored data can be <u>vulnerable</u> to hackers (p77).
- Unclear who has <u>ownership</u> over cloud data.
- Subscription fees for using cloud <u>storage</u> may be expensive in the <u>long term</u>.

A quick Summary...

It can get pretty confusing with all this 'thingy is faster than thingy which is cheaper than thingy but holds less than thingy'. So here's a summary of relative <u>speeds</u>, <u>costs</u> and <u>capacities</u>.

Optical Disc	Memory Card		Magnetic Tape	HDD		SSD
Slowest		**Average read/write speed**				*Fastest*

Magnetic Tape		Optical Disc	HDD		Memory Card	SSD
Cheapest		**Average cost (per GB)**				*Priciest*

Optical Disc	Memory Card	SSD		HDD		Magnetic Tape
Lowest		**Average capacity**				*Highest*

The speed, cost and capacity of cloud storage depends a lot on the service and on your Internet connection.

Harder, Better, Faster, Stronger... cheaper, more reliable... more shiny...

Poor old optical discs. I remember when this happened to Mr Floppy. It made me very sad...
Here's Mr Floppy with his remarkable 1.44 MB of storage.

System Software — The OS

System software is software designed to run and maintain a computer system. By far the most important one is the operating system (OS). There's also utility programs (p59) but those are very much the runners-up.

Operating Systems *manage* Hardware *and run* Software

An Operating System (OS) is a complex piece of software found on most computer systems. The main functions of an OS are to:

- Communicate with input and output devices via device drivers.
- Provide a platform for applications to run on, and a user interface.
- Control memory management and allocation.
- Organise the CPU and its processing tasks.
- Deal with file management and disk management.
- Manage system security and user accounts.

Let's look at each function in a bit more detail...

The OS *Communicates* with I/O Devices *through Drivers*

I/O (input/output) devices allow computers to take inputs (e.g. through a keyboard, microphone, webcam, etc.) and give outputs (e.g. through a monitor, speakers, printer, etc.). Operating systems use device drivers to communicate with I/O devices connected to the computer system:

- Every I/O device connected to the computer system requires a device driver. Drivers essentially act as a 'translator' for the signals between the OS and the device.
- When a computer is booted up, the OS will choose the correct device drivers for the device it detects. If new devices are connected to the computer, the system may automatically find and install a new, matching driver.
- Device manufacturers may release updates to device drivers in order to fix bugs, add features or improve the performance of their device. Updates may be installed automatically by the OS or manually by the user.

The OS also manages *Applications*

1) Operating systems provide a platform for applications to run on, and manage system resources (see next page) to allow computers to run multiple applications at once — known as multitasking.

2) It also allows applications to access hardware and other peripheral devices as needed, including access to RAM (see next page) and secondary storage (e.g. so files can be opened and saved).

3) The OS also provides a user interface that applications are accessed through. Most desktop computers traditionally use graphical interfaces (GUIs) that are WIMP-based, where applications are displayed with windows, icons, menus and pointers.

4) These interfaces are ideal for use with a mouse and keyboard, but devices with different input methods (e.g. smartphones with touchscreens) may have very different interfaces.

5) Applications are usually written for a particular OS and will take advantage of its features, e.g. using standard windows and menus in a WIMP interface, or allowing users to tap, pinch and swipe on a touchscreen device.

©iStock.com/valio84sl

You can swipe between screens or tap an icon to open it on Android™.

A driver lets a computer speak to a mouse? If you say so...

Remember, the OS is the boss of the computer system. It controls hardware via drivers, allows the computer to run applications and gives you an interface to interact with them through. So yeah, it's important. Make sure you've got your head round everything on this page before moving on.

System Software — The OS

The OS is in charge of Memory Management

1) When an application is <u>opened</u>, the OS copies the <u>necessary</u> parts of the application to <u>memory</u>, followed by <u>additional</u> parts when they are required. The OS will decide if applications or features have been used recently — if <u>not</u>, they may be <u>removed</u> from memory.

2) The OS manages <u>how much</u> RAM a program has access to. This will depend on the program — for example, <u>image editing</u> software usually uses a lot of memory, while <u>text editors</u> need much less RAM. Certain things, like having <u>more documents</u> open, can make a program require <u>additional memory</u>.

3) When running <u>multiple</u> applications at once, the OS makes sure that they <u>don't overwrite</u> or <u>interfere</u> with each other by allocating certain applications certain memory addresses, keeping their processes in separate locations.

The OS tells the CPU what to Process

System software also creates processes, which run in the background.

1) When an application is <u>launched</u>, it creates one or more <u>processes</u>. Each process has instructions that it needs the CPU to execute. However, CPUs can only carry out instructions from <u>one process</u> at a time.

2) <u>Operating systems</u> deal with this by using <u>scheduling</u> to determine the <u>most efficient order</u> for the CPU to execute instructions.

3) Each process is allocated a '<u>priority</u>' by the OS. The CPU carries out the instructions from the highest-priority processes first, and the other processes <u>wait</u> in a queue.

4) The OS may interrupt the current CPU process if a higher-priority process becomes available.

5) In order to allow <u>multitasking</u>, the CPU <u>swaps between</u> different processes <u>very rapidly</u> — remember, most CPUs can carry out <u>billions</u> of instructions in a second (p54).

What time do you call this, Mr Process?

It won't happen again, Mr CPU sir.

The OS handles File and Disk Management

1) Computers store data as <u>files</u>. Images, music, videos and spreadsheets are all just collections of data. <u>File extensions</u> (for example .jpg, .mp3, .mpeg) tell the computer which <u>software</u> should be used to open the file.

2) The OS is responsible for <u>file management</u> — the organisation of data into a usable <u>hierarchical structure</u>. It also deals with the <u>movement</u>, <u>editing</u> and <u>deletion</u> of data.

3) The OS manages the <u>hard disk</u>. It splits the <u>physical disk</u> into storage <u>sectors</u>, decides which sectors to <u>write data</u> to, and keeps track of <u>free space</u> on the disk. Ideally, the data for a <u>single</u> file would be placed in <u>adjacent</u> sectors, but this isn't always possible (p59).

Utilities like <u>File Explorer</u> allow users to <u>navigate</u> and <u>edit</u> the file structure or access their files.

4) The OS also organises and maintains the hard disk with <u>utility programs</u> (see p59) like <u>defragmentation software</u>.

Operating Systems manage System Security

1) Most popular OSs include ways of keeping data stored on a system <u>secure</u>. One common way in which they do this is through <u>user account control</u>. User accounts allow different users to be <u>granted</u> or <u>denied access</u> to specific data or resources on a computer system.

2) On most desktop operating systems, each user has access to <u>their own personal data</u> and <u>desktop</u>, but cannot access other users' personal data, unless they are a <u>system administrator</u>.

3) Operating systems may have <u>anti-theft measures</u> to prevent other users from accessing locked devices or accounts to steal information. User accounts may be <u>password</u>, or <u>pin</u> protected. Some devices also require a user to draw a specific <u>pattern</u> on the screen, or have <u>fingerprint</u> or <u>retina</u> scanners.

Now, if only my OS could manage my washing up for me too...

If you didn't believe me before that the OS is incredibly important, I bet you do now. Once you're done learning this page, go say thank you to your OS for everything it does for you. It deserves some love.

System Software — Utilities

Operating systems are amazing things, but they'd be less amazing without the tools of their trade — utilities.

Utilities *help to* Maintain *a computer*

Utility programs are used to maintain or configure a computer. Many useful utilities are installed with the operating system, but you can install other ones to perform additional tasks.

Defragmentation

Files are stored on a hard disk in available spaces. Ideally, whole files would be stored together, but as files are moved and deleted, gaps appear on the disk. The OS has to split new files up to fill the gaps. This makes reading these files slower as the read/write head has to move back and forth across the disk. Defragmentation puts the files back into one block and collects the free space together:

Each colour is a file — Data on HDD | Gaps appear — Files deleted | New file (grey) split into blocks. — New file added | Blocks collected Gaps collected — After defragmentation

As SSDs have no moving parts, fragmentation doesn't slow them down — in fact, defragmenting them can actually shorten their lifespan.

Disk Health

Over time, hard drives can start to deteriorate, causing corrupted data and slow read/write speeds. Disk health utilities scan the drive for problems and fix issues where possible.

Compression

Compression software reduces the size of files so they take up less disk space (see p46). It's used loads on the Internet to make files quicker to download. Standard file formats include .zip and .rar. Compressed files need to be extracted before they can be used.

Encryption

Encryption software (see p72) scrambles (encrypts) data to stop third-parties from accessing it. Encrypted data can be decrypted using a special 'key'.

Backup

A backup is a copy of a computer system's files and settings stored externally that can be restored in the event of data loss. Data loss can happen for many reasons — fire, theft, flood, malware, hardware failure, or 'oops I accidentally selected all and pressed delete'. A backup utility is software with facilities such as scheduling of regular backups, creating rescue disks, disk images, and options for how much data to backup.

Cause of data loss #433

Virus Scanners

These inspect each file on your computer, looking for viruses. They usually have a list of known viruses to check for — they need to be updated regularly so they don't miss anything.

System Cleanup

Programs like web browsers leave a lot of temporary files on your hard drive, which can end up taking up lots of space unnecessarily. System cleanup utilities go through and get rid of files like these.

Utilities — exactly what they say on the tin...

Remember, utilities are bits of software that help maintain your system. There are plenty more you could mention in the exam, e.g. system restore, file managers, antispyware, firewalls, software auto-update, etc.

Translators

Programmers often use application software (such as Microsoft Visual Studio®) to help them to write code. This software usually includes translators to turn the code they write into a form a computer can understand.

Computer Languages can be High-Level or Low-Level

1) Most of the programming languages that you'll be familiar with (e.g. Python®, C#) are high-level languages. The source code is easy for humans to write, but computers need to translate it (see below) before they can read and run it.

2) On the other hand, low-level languages are tricky for humans to read and write but are easier for a computer to run. They consist of machine code and assembly languages:

```
000000 00010 00011 00100 00000 100000
```
Machine code is very tricky for humans to understand. Each processor (or family of processors) will have its own specific machine code.

```
ADD r4, r2, r3
```
Assembly code is more readable for humans and easier to remember, so programmers are less likely to make mistakes writing assembly code than machine code. It's often used when developing software for embedded systems (see p50) and when programmers need more control over specific hardware.

3) High-level languages are popular with programmers, but low-level languages have their uses too:

High-Level Languages	Low-Level Languages
• One instruction of high-level code represents many instructions of machine code.	• One instruction of assembly code usually only represents one instruction of machine code.
• The same code will work for many different machines and processors.	• Usually written for one type of machine or processor and won't work on any others.
• The programmer can easily store data in lots of different structures (e.g. lists and arrays) without knowing about the memory structure.	• The programmer needs to know about the internal structure of the CPU (see p51-52) and how it manages the memory.
• Code is easy to read, understand and modify.	• Code is very difficult to read, understand and modify.
• Must be translated before a computer is able to understand it.	• Commands in machine code can be executed directly without the need for a translator.
• You don't have much control over what the CPU actually does so programs will be less memory efficient and slower.	• You control exactly what the CPU does and how it uses memory so programs will be more memory efficient and faster.

High-Level and Assembly Languages need to be Translated

1) Computers only understand instructions given to them as machine code, so high level languages and assembly languages need to be translated before a computer is able to execute the instructions.

2) There are three types of translator that you need to know about: assemblers, compilers and interpreters.

3) Assemblers translate assembly languages directly into machine code. There are many different assembly languages (to support different CPU types) and each one needs its own unique assembler.

4) Compilers translate high-level code directly into machine code, and create an executable file.

5) Interpreters don't translate directly into machine code — instead, they take each instruction in the code and call machine code subroutines within their own code to carry out that instruction.

Compiler	Interpreter
Translates all of the source code at the same time and creates one executable file.	Translates and runs the source code one instruction at a time, but doesn't create an executable file.
Only needed once to create the executable file.	Needed every time you want to run the program.
Returns a list of errors for the entire program once compiling is complete.	The interpreter will return the first error it finds and then stop — this is useful for debugging.
Once compiled the program runs quickly, but compiling can take a long time.	Programs will run more slowly because the code is being translated as the program is running.

"Cette page est incroyable!" — call in the translators...

Sometimes programmers may want to use a specific type of translator. For example, interpreters are often used when you're developing software, and compilers are used when you want to distribute software.

Relational Databases

Databases are used to store large amounts of data. They make retrieving information easy and efficient.

Databases *organise data into Fields and Records*

1) Databases store data in <u>tables</u>
   — the <u>columns</u> of these tables
   are called <u>fields</u> and the <u>rows</u>
   of the tables are called <u>records</u>.

2) A field is used to store a <u>specific piece</u>
   <u>of information</u>, e.g. a name or address.
   A record then uses the fields to <u>store details</u>
   about a <u>specific item</u> — there's more about records on page 20.

3) Each field has a specific <u>data type</u> (see p8) assigned to it
   — for example, the 'numberOfStaff' field would be an <u>integer</u>.

4) Each table in a database has a <u>primary key</u>. A primary key is a field which can
   <u>uniquely identify</u> any record in the table. There can only be <u>one</u> primary key field per database table.

Primary key → Each column is a field. Field name →

Each row → is a record.

siteID	department	numberOfStaff	phoneNumber
1	Editing	113	01632 960378
2	Packing	36	01632 960549
3	Production	12	01632 960912

Databases can be *Flat-file or Relational*

1) <u>Flat-file databases</u> store all the data in <u>one table</u>, which makes them simple to <u>set up</u> and <u>understand</u>.

2) <u>Relational databases</u> can be more complicated — they are made up of <u>multiple</u> tables that
   are often linked together using <u>primary keys</u> (see above) and <u>foreign keys</u> (see below).

3) A foreign key is a <u>field</u> that references the <u>primary key</u> of another table.
   This creates a <u>link</u> between two tables, as shown below.

Ciao!

Hallo!

Bonjour!

Table: customers

customerID	name	emailAddress
1	Kalika	koolkalika@azmail.co.uk
2	Siwan	supersiwan@azmail.co.uk
3	Fran	fabfran@azmail.co.uk

In the 'customers'
table customerID
is the primary key.

Table: orders

orderID	customerID	amount
001	2	£212
002	1	£855
003	2	£629

In the 'orders' table orderID is the primary key.

The customerID field is a foreign key in this table — it links
each record in this table to a record in the 'customers' table.
Note, values in a foreign key field <u>do not</u> have to be unique.

Having the same piece of data stored in multiple places is called
data redundancy — it can cause big problems for large databases.

Advantages of Relational Databases

- Data is only stored in <u>one place</u> and then <u>referenced</u>. This means that to input, update or
  delete a piece of data it only has to be done in <u>one place</u> which can <u>prevent inconsistencies</u>.
  In the example above, if the <u>name</u> and <u>emailAddress</u> fields were stored in the <u>orders table</u> then
  <u>Siwan's</u> name and email address would have to be entered <u>twice</u> as she placed <u>two orders</u>.

- Only storing the same piece of data once will also <u>save storage space</u>.

- Relational databases can be <u>more secure</u> — some tables can be made
  <u>confidential</u> so only <u>some users</u> can see certain data. In the example above,
  someone working in customer services might need access to <u>both tables</u>,
  whereas a warehouse worker might only need access to the <u>orders table</u>.

Secure databases can
help companies to
meet data protection
laws (see p77).

After the relationship ended, Dave the Database began to feel flat...

Databases are a useful way of storing large amounts of data in one organised structure. They are often
used on websites that require users to log on — they store details about the user like their username.

SQL

Structured Query Language (SQL) can be used to search the tables of a database for specific data. When we talk about the records and fields of a database table we just mean the rows and columns.

SELECT and FROM are the most important keywords

To write a <u>query</u> that <u>retrieves</u> data from a database, use the <u>SELECT</u> keyword followed by the names of the <u>fields</u> (columns) you to want to <u>retrieve</u> and <u>display</u>. Then use the <u>FROM</u> keyword followed by the name of the <u>table</u> (or <u>tables</u>) you want to search.

Table: hotels

ID	hotelName	hotelRating	rooms	bathroom	priceInPounds
1	Water Lodge	2.3	50	En-suite	42
2	Fire Inn	4.2	64	Shared	42
3	Earthen House	4.4	215	En-suite	39
4	Windy Hotel	3.5	150	Shared	57
5	River Hotel	3.8	180	Shared	46

```
SELECT hotelName
FROM hotels
```
This returns hotelName for all the records in the table hotels.

```
SELECT hotelName, hotelRating
FROM hotels
```
This returns hotelName and hotelRating for all the records in the table hotels.

```
SELECT *
FROM hotels
```
If you want to return all the fields, you can use * as a wildcard.

You can use WHERE to filter the results

1) The <u>WHERE</u> keyword is used to specify <u>conditions</u> that a record must satisfy to be returned.

```
SELECT * FROM hotels WHERE hotelRating >= 4.1
```

* is the wildcard character and will return all the fields.

Look in the table hotels.

This condition looks for records with a hotelRating greater than or equal to 4.1.

ID	hotelName	hotelRating	rooms	bathroom	priceInPounds
2	Fire Inn	4.2	64	Shared	42
3	Earthen House	4.4	215	En-suite	39

The specified fields of the records that satisfy the condition are then returned.

2) The Boolean operators <u>AND</u> and <u>OR</u> can be used with <u>WHERE</u> to make more <u>specific searches</u>.

```
SELECT hotelName FROM hotels WHERE bathroom = "En-suite" AND priceInPounds < 45
```

Will only select the hotelName.

Look in the table hotels.

This condition uses a Boolean operator to check if a hotel room has an en-suite bathroom AND is less than £45.

hotelName
Water Lodge
Earthen House

You can also ORDER data before it is returned

In SQL the <u>ORDER BY</u> keyword is used to sort records into ascending (ASC) or descending (DESC) order.

EXAMPLE: Stacey is searching for a hotel that has more than 100 rooms but she doesn't want to stay in the Windy Hotel. Write a search query for Stacey that returns the name and price of the hotels that match her requirements. The information should be sorted by price from high to low.

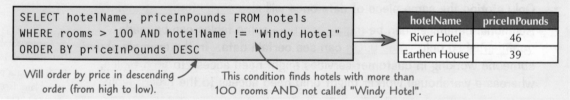

```
SELECT hotelName, priceInPounds FROM hotels
WHERE rooms > 100 AND hotelName != "Windy Hotel"
ORDER BY priceInPounds DESC
```

hotelName	priceInPounds
River Hotel	46
Earthen House	39

Will order by price in descending order (from high to low).

This condition finds hotels with more than 100 rooms AND not called "Windy Hotel".

*SELECT * FROM images WHERE category = "Surprised Animals"...*

The commands and syntax in SQL are so easy you'll be able to pick it up in no time. Make sure you know how to use the SELECT, FROM, WHERE and ORDER BY keywords, including the use of *.

SQL

Most Databases use SQL to manage them

1) You can add records to a table by using the keywords **INSERT INTO** and **VALUES**:

```
INSERT INTO hotels VALUES
(6, "Lighten Inn", 4.8, 125, "En-suite", 50)
```

When you're inserting complete records into a table there is no need to specify the fields you want to store the data values in.

```
INSERT INTO hotels (ID, hotelName, bathroom)
VALUES (7, "Hail Inn", "En-suite")
```

When you aren't inserting a complete record you'll have to specify the fields you want to assign the values to.

2) To update records you can use **UPDATE**, **SET** and **WHERE**.

```
UPDATE hotels SET priceInPounds = 21, hotelRating = 3.5 WHERE ID = 3
```

The table you want to update.

The fields you want to change and the values you want to change them to.

The condition that determines which records will be updated. If you're updating a single record, it's often best to use the primary key field.

3) To delete records you can use **DELETE**, **FROM** and **WHERE**.

```
DELETE FROM hotels WHERE hotelRating = 2.3
```

The table you want to delete a record from.

The condition that determines which records are deleted.

If multiple records satisfy the condition, then all of those records will be updated or deleted.

You can also Retrieve Data from Relational Databases

EXAMPLE: An estate agency uses a relational database to store information about viewings and properties. The database includes two tables called "viewings" and "properties", shown below. Write an SQL query that returns the addresses and times of all viewings with "Helen". The information should be returned in time order from earliest to latest.

viewings

viewing	customer	propertyNumber	time
01	Helen	3	11:45
02	Sadik	2	10:15
03	Helen	2	09:30

The propertyNumber field is the viewings table's foreign key and the properties table's primary key (see page 61).

properties

propertyNumber	parking	address
1	Street	61 Roman Rd, Leeds, LS2 2EH
2	Driveway	12 Greek Lane, Leeds, LS2 5ZN
3	Street	33 Viking Street, Leeds, LS1 8UU

SELECT the relevant fields and include both table names after the FROM keyword.

Writing fields as tableName.fieldName makes it clear which table the field is from.

```
SELECT properties.address, viewings.time
FROM properties, viewings
WHERE viewings.propertyNumber = properties.propertyNumber
AND customer = "Helen"
ORDER BY time ASC
```

You need to include both table names in the FROM statement.

This condition joins the two tables by matching the propertyNumber field.

This will order the results by time in ascending order (from earliest to latest).

Now that the tables are joined, this condition finds the records that have "Helen" as a customer.

address	time
12 Greek Lane, Leeds, LS2 5ZN	09:30
33 Viking Street, Leeds, LS1 8UU	11:45

This is the result of the SQL query.

INSERT INTO page VALUES (awful joke with tenuous link to page)

When tables are joined together (like in the WHERE clause of the example above), rows from the two tables are combined based on a key field. This allows you to use and return fields from both tables in a single query.

Revision Questions for Section Five

Well, that wraps up Section 5. You should be an expert on computer systems now, but we'd better just check:
- Try these questions and tick off each one when you get it right.
- When you've done all the questions for a topic and are completely happy with it, tick off the topic.

Computer Systems and the CPU (p50-52) ☑

1) Define hardware and software.
2) Give one example of system software and one example of application software.
3) What is: a) an embedded system?   b) a control system?
4) Explain the role of the control unit in the CPU.
5) What does ALU stand for and what does it do?
6) What is cache and what is it used for?
7) Describe what happens at each stage of the CPU fetch-execute cycle.

Memory and Computer Performance (p53-54) ☑

8) What's the difference between volatile and non-volatile memory?
9) What does RAM stand for? Describe how RAM is used in a computer system.
10) Could changing the amount of RAM affect the performance of the computer? Explain your answer.
11) Explain why ROM is required by a computer system.
12) Name three characteristics of a processor that may affect its performance.

Secondary Storage (p55-56) ☑

13) Define primary and secondary storage and give an example of each.
14) Who would win in a fight between an HDD and SSD? Give a blow by blow commentary of the match.
15) Why might someone choose magnetic tape as a form of storage?
16) What are the pros and cons of: a) optical discs?   b) cloud storage?
17) Draw a diagram to summarise cost, speed and capacity for different types of secondary storage.

System Software (p57-59) ☑

18) List six functions of an operating system.
19) Explain how device drivers are used in a computer system.
20) Describe how the OS manages: a) memory   b) the CPU   c) files and disk space
21) Give three ways in which an OS might keep your files secure.
22) List seven types of utility program and explain what they do.

Translators (p60) ☑

23) Define and give an example of the following: a) Machine code   b) Assembly Language
24) Give six differences between high-level languages and low-level languages.
25) What are the three types of translator?
26) Compare the functionality and uses of a compiler and an interpreter.

Relational Databases and SQL (p61-63) ☑

27) In a database, what is: a) a field?   b) a record?   c) a primary key?   d) a foreign key?
28) What is the difference between a flat-file database and a relational database?
29)*Outline what the following SQL query would do:

```
SELECT name FROM staff WHERE salary >= 35000 ORDER BY salary ASC
```

*Answer on p81

Networks

When you connect a device to another one, you're creating a network — networks allow devices to share information and resources. Here we'll look at the types of network you'll need to know for your exam.

A LAN is a Local Area Network

1) A LAN covers a <u>small geographical area</u> located on a <u>single site</u>.
2) All the hardware for a LAN is <u>owned</u> by the organisation that uses it.
3) LANs can be <u>wired</u> (e.g. with <u>Ethernet</u> cables) or <u>wireless</u> — see next page.
4) You'll often find LANs in <u>businesses</u>, <u>schools</u> and <u>universities</u>.
5) Lots of homes have a LAN to connect various devices, such as <u>PCs</u>, <u>tablets</u>, <u>smart TVs</u> and <u>printers</u>.

A WAN is a network that Connects LANs

1) WAN stands for <u>Wide Area Network</u>. A WAN connects LANs that are in <u>different geographical locations</u>. For example, a business with offices in three different countries would need a WAN for all their devices to connect together.
2) Unlike a LAN, organisations <u>hire infrastructure</u> (e.g. communication lines) from telecommunications companies, who own and manage the WAN. This is because a WAN is much more <u>expensive</u> to set up than a LAN.
3) WANs may be connected using <u>telephone lines</u> (copper or fibre optic), <u>satellite links</u> or <u>radio links</u>.
4) The <u>Internet</u> is, of course, the biggest WAN (and in my opinion, the best).

A PAN is a Personal Network

1) <u>Personal Area Networks</u> (PANs) connect devices over a <u>very short range</u>. They're normally centred around a <u>single user</u>, and are often used to transmit between mobile/wearable devices (e.g. smartphones, smartwatches, headphones, etc.).
2) PANs often use common wireless technology (e.g. <u>Bluetooth</u>®) to connect devices. A Bluetooth® signal is <u>quite strong</u>, but has a very <u>short range</u> which makes it ideal for connecting devices in the <u>same room</u>.
3) PANs are handy as they usually <u>don't</u> require any <u>additional hardware</u>, just the devices themselves. This also means you can create a PAN <u>on the move</u>.

Networking Computers has Benefits and Drawbacks

BENEFITS

1) <u>Sharing files</u> is easier — network users can access the same files, <u>work on them</u> at the same time and <u>copy files</u> between machines.
2) You can share the same <u>hardware</u> (like <u>printers</u>) between multiple devices.
3) You can install and update <u>software</u> on all computers at once, rather than one-by-one.
4) You can <u>communicate</u> across a network <u>cheaply</u> and <u>easily</u>, e.g. with <u>email</u>.
5) <u>User accounts</u> can be stored centrally, so users can <u>log in</u> from <u>any device</u> on the network.

DRAWBACKS

1) They can be <u>expensive</u> to set up, as you often need a lot of extra <u>hardware</u> (see next page).
2) Networks can be <u>vulnerable</u> to <u>hacking</u> (see p77), and <u>malware</u> (p70) can easily spread between networked computers.
3) Some networks are <u>dependent</u> on one or more <u>servers</u> (see p67). If those servers go down it can be very <u>disruptive</u> for people trying to use the network.
4) Large networks are <u>difficult to manage</u> and may require employing a <u>specialist</u> to maintain them.

Don't LANguish at the bottom of the class — learn this page...

Right then. Make sure you're absolutely clear about the differences between the three types of network before moving on. Remember, companies use their own cables for LANs, but they hire lines for WANs. And if you forget about PANs, the PANstrosity will find you and sink its grisly blue tooth into you...

Networks — Wired and Wireless

Connecting devices doesn't magically happen. To create a network, you usually need certain pieces of hardware...

Networks require lots of Hardware

1) A <u>Network Interface Card</u> (NIC) is a piece of hardware inside a device that allows it to connect to networks. NICs exist for both <u>wired</u> and <u>wireless</u> connections.

2) <u>Switches</u> are used to <u>connect devices</u> on a LAN, while <u>routers</u> transmit data between <u>different networks</u>, and are most commonly used to connect to the <u>Internet</u>. Most home 'routers' are in fact a router, switch and WAP (see below) <u>all-in-one</u>.

3) Wired networks can use different <u>cables</u> to connect devices — the choice of cable usually depends on <u>cost</u>, <u>bandwidth</u> and how far you want to <u>transmit data</u>.

<u>Bandwidth</u> is the amount of data that can be sent across a network in a given time.

- <u>Fibre optic</u> cables transmit data as <u>light</u>. They are <u>high performance</u> and <u>expensive</u> cables — they don't suffer <u>interference</u> and can transmit over <u>very large distances</u> at a <u>high bandwidth</u> without loss of signal quality.

- <u>CAT 5e</u> and <u>CAT 6</u> are common types of <u>Ethernet</u> cable. They contain pairs of <u>copper wires</u> which are twisted together to reduce internal <u>interference</u>. They're <u>cheaper</u> than fibre optic cables and have a <u>decent bandwidth</u>, which is why they're commonly used in homes and offices to connect devices on a LAN.

- <u>Coaxial</u> cables are made of a <u>single copper wire</u> surrounded by a plastic layer for insulation and a metallic mesh which provides <u>shielding</u> from <u>outside interference</u>. They tend to be <u>very cheap</u>, although they also have a <u>low bandwidth</u>.

Twisted pair of copper wires

CAT 6 cable

Metallic mesh
Copper wire
Insulation
Coaxial cable

Wireless Networks use Radio Waves to transmit data

1) Local wireless networks are called <u>WLANs</u> (wireless LANs). Most people refer to these as <u>Wi-Fi</u>®, but Wi-Fi® is actually a specific <u>family</u> of WLAN <u>protocols</u> (see p69).

2) Like mobile phones and TVs, wireless networks use <u>radio waves</u> to transmit data.

3) To set up a wireless network, you need a <u>Wireless Access Point (WAP)</u> device. The WAP is basically a <u>switch</u> that allows devices to connect wirelessly.

4) Don't confuse WAPs with <u>hotspots</u> — <u>locations</u> where you can connect to a WAP.

5) To connect, devices need <u>wireless capability</u>. This is built-in to many devices these days, but if not, you can use a <u>USB dongle</u>.

Ralf and Rory chillaxing on a pair of dongles.

Wireless networks have benefits and drawbacks when compared to wired networks:

BENEFITS OF WIRELESS NETWORKS	DRAWBACKS OF WIRELESS NETWORKS
1) Wireless networks are <u>convenient</u>, as you can get your device to <u>automatically connect</u> to the network, and can also <u>move around</u> while connected to the network.	1) Wireless networks are generally <u>less secure</u> than wired networks — access points are usually visible to <u>all devices</u>, not just trusted ones, which can allow hackers to gain access.
2) They can be <u>cheaper</u> and better for the <u>environment</u> as you don't need any <u>wires</u>.	2) <u>Distance</u> from the WAP, <u>interference</u> from other wireless networks, and physical <u>obstructions</u> (e.g. walls) can all <u>reduce signal strength</u>. This means there's a <u>limit</u> on <u>how far</u> a wireless network can <u>reach</u>.
3) It's very easy to <u>add more users</u> to a wireless network — you don't need to install <u>extra wires</u> or do any <u>complex setup</u>.	3) They generally have a <u>lower bandwidth</u> and are <u>less reliable</u> than wired networks.

Hardware — nothing to do with concrete jackets...

In your exam, you might have to compare fibre optic and copper cables (which include CAT5e/6 and coaxial). You could also be asked which you think is more suited to a given situation. You should think in terms of cost (fibre optic = expensive, copper = cheap) and speed (fibre optic = fast, copper = slow).

Network Topologies

A topology is essentially the layout of the network. Networks can be arranged in lots of different topologies, but star and bus are the two important ones you'll need to know for the exam.

In a *Star Topology* all devices are connected to the centre

In a star topology, all the devices are connected to a central switch or server that controls the network.

STAR Server Switch

The central switch allows many devices to access the server simultaneously.

Star networks may be wired or wireless.

Pros

- If a device fails or a cable is disconnected, the rest of the network is unaffected.
- It's simple to add more devices to the network, since each device is connected to the switch using a separate cable.
- Star topologies tend to have better performance than other setups — data goes straight to the central device so all devices can transmit data at the same time.
- There are very few data collisions on a star network compared with other network topologies (e.g. bus).

Cons

- In wired networks, every device needs a cable to connect to the central switch or server. This can be expensive, e.g. for an office building with 50 terminals.
- The switch itself is also an expensive piece of hardware.
- If there is a problem with the switch or server then the whole network is affected.
- The maximum number of possible connections on the network is determined by the switch — if you need more, you might need to buy a new one.

In a *Bus Topology* all devices are connected to a *Single Cable*

1) Bus topologies use a single 'backbone' cable, called a bus, to connect all the devices.

2) Two terminators are placed at the ends of the bus to stop data ~~getting to Sarah Connor~~ reflecting back along the bus. Without the terminators, reflected signals would cause interference and potentially make the network unusable.

Backbone cable Terminator Terminator Server **BUS**

Pros

- Like in a star topology, the network is unaffected if a device fails.
- Bus networks aren't dependent on a central switch working to keep the whole network running.
- They're relatively cheap to set up compared to star networks. The total length of wiring needed is much less, and the hardware you need (the bus cable and terminators) is cheaper than switches, both to buy and to maintain.

Cons

- Data collisions are common on a bus network. When there is a data collision the data must be resent, which slows the network down.
- The more devices you add to the network, the more likely data collisions are. This makes bus topologies unsuitable for large networks.
- To try and avoid data collisions, devices must wait for the bus to be available before they can send any data — this can also slow the network down.
- If the bus cable gets broken (e.g. from nibbling rats), it splits the network into separate parts. Since the separated networks don't have terminators at both ends of the bus, there will be a lot of reflected signals which can shut down the entire network.

"You can't handle a bus network — you've got no backbone"...

Star networks are pretty common, but the fact that they rely on the central switch can cause all sorts of problems if the switch fails. Bus topologies are usually cheaper, but they can be really slow when there's heavy traffic — just like real buses. And if you'd like more driving similes, just keep reading.

Network Protocols

Moving data on the network is like going on a car journey — you need a destination, something to tell you how to get there, and rules to stop you crashing into anyone else on the road. That's where protocols come in.

Networks need Protocols to set the rules

1) A protocol is a set of rules for how devices communicate and how data is transmitted across a network.
2) Protocols cover how communication between two devices should start and end, how the data should be organised, and what the devices should do if data goes missing.
3) Data sent between networks is split into equal-sized packets. Each packet contains extra information like the destination and source addresses (see next page) and a checksum (used to find errors).

Network protocols are divided into Layers

to make the ultimate cake

1) A layer is a group of protocols which have similar functions.
2) Layers are self-contained — protocols in each layer do their job without needing to know what's happening in the other layers.

Data can only be passed between adjacent layers. E.g. Layer 2 can pass data to Layers 1 and 3 but Layer 1 can only pass data to Layer 2.

3) Each layer serves the layer above it — it does the hidden work needed for an action on the layer above. E.g. when you send an email (on layer 4), this triggers actions in layer 3, which triggers actions in layer 2, all the way down to layer 1.
4) The four layers of the TCP/IP model are shown below:

	Layer Name	Protocols in this layer cover...	Protocol examples
icing			
avocado	Layer 4 — Application Layer	Providing networking services to applications — e.g. turning data into websites.	HTTP, HTTPS, FTP, SMTP, IMAP
lemon	Layer 3 — Transport Layer	Setting up communications between two devices, splitting data into packets and checking packets are correctly sent and delivered.	TCP, UDP
orange	Layer 2 — Internet Layer	Adding IP addresses to data packets, directing them between devices and handling traffic. Used by routers.	IP
strawberry	Layer 1 — Link Layer	Passing data over the physical network. Responsible for how data is sent as electrical signals over cables, wireless and other hardware, e.g. NICs (p66), and for interpreting signals using device drivers (p57).	Wi-Fi®, Ethernet

ADVANTAGES OF USING LAYERS

1) It breaks network communication into manageable pieces. This helps developers concentrate on only one area of the network without having to worry about the others.
2) As layers are self-contained, they can be changed without the other layers being affected.
3) Having set rules for each layer forces companies to make compatible, universal hardware and software, so different brands will work with each other and always work in basically the same way.

Lots of Important Protocols work on the Application Layer

In the TCP/IP model, the application layer is responsible for things like file, email and data transfer:

Protocol	Stands for...	What is it used for?
HTTP	Hyper Text Transfer Protocol	Used by web browsers to access websites and communicate with web servers.
HTTPS	HTTP Secure	A more secure version of HTTP. Encrypts all information sent and received.
FTP	File Transfer Protocol	Used to access, edit and move files between devices on a network, e.g. to access files on a server from a client computer.
IMAP	Internet Message Access Protocol	Used to retrieve emails from a server.
SMTP	Simple Mail Transfer Protocol	Used to send emails. Also used to transfer emails between servers.

Protocols are like onions — they make me cry...

At least, I think that's why they're like onions. Anyway, there's lots of stuff to learn here — make sure you know what layers are, why they're useful and what all those different application layer protocols are for.

Network Protocols

TCP and UDP split the data into Packets

1) TCP and UDP are transport layer protocols which control the packaging and unpackaging of data.

2) Transmission Control Protocol (TCP) establishes a connection between the sending and receiving devices. It then splits the data into numbered packets that can be reassembled into the original data once they reach their destination, even if they arrive out of order.

3) It communicates with the receiving device to make sure that all packets have been transferred correctly. If not, the missing/corrupted packets can be resent. The sending device gets confirmation when the transfer is complete.

4) User Datagram Protocol (UDP) breaks the data down into packets without numbering them. They are read by the receiving device in the order that they arrive — even if that's not the order they were sent.

5) UDP only sends each packet once and doesn't check with the receiving device that everything has been received. This saves time, but there's no way of knowing if packets have gone missing in transit.

6) UDP is suitable for applications that need fast, efficient transmission, e.g. live video streaming. A hiccup in video quality from a missing packet is better than a delay in the live stream.

7) TCP is better when you need a reliable connection, e.g. downloading files. Missing data packets can cause files to be corrupted and unusable, but you wouldn't want to have to redownload the whole file.

IP is responsible for Packet Switching

1) Internet Protocol (IP) operates on the Internet layer, establishing connections between routers and handling network traffic. IP addresses are unique numbers assigned to every device connected to an IP network — they are added to the header of each packet at the Internet layer.

2) IP is responsible for directing data packets to their destination across the Internet or other IP networks using a process called packet switching.

3) Each packet is sent between a series of routers — each router reads the packet's header and uses the IP address to decide which router to send the packet to next.

He he he...

4) Which way the data is sent changes depending on network traffic — so the packets can take different routes. If a router receives too many packets at once, it may prioritise some over others.

5) Packet switching is an efficient use of the network because there are so many possible routes that each packet can take — packets can reach their receiving device quickly, even if there's heavy traffic.

Wi-Fi® is the Standard set of Protocols for Wireless LANs

1) Like we mentioned on p66, Wi-Fi® is a family of protocols commonly used in WLANs. It operates on the link layer — units of data sent on the link layer are called frames instead of packets.

2) Wi-Fi® uses two radio frequency bands — 2.4 GHz and 5 GHz. 2.4 GHz has a greater range and is better at getting through walls and other obstructions, while 5 GHz is faster over short distances.

Channels
1 2 3 4 5...

3) The bands are split into numbered channels that each cover a small frequency range. The channels in the 2.4 GHz band overlap. Networks using adjacent or overlapping channels can cause interference.

2.4 GHz   2.42 GHz   2.44 GHz

4) It's important that data is encrypted (see p72) on Wi-Fi® networks. There are security protocols for this, such as WPA™ (Wi-Fi® Protected Access).

Wi-Fi® and Ethernet use switches to direct data frames to a device using its MAC address (p72).

ETHERNET IS USED ON WIRED NETWORKS

Ethernet is another family of protocols that operates on the link layer. Like Wi-Fi®, it also handles the transmission of data between devices on LANs, but Ethernet is specifically for wired connections.

I ended up with the wrong router — the packets were switched...

IP addresses usually look something like 37.153.62.136. They can be static (you get the same one every time you connect to a network) or dynamic (you can get a different one each time you connect to a network).

Cyber Security Threats

Networks are great for lots of reasons, but they can also cause a lot of headaches. Hackers and criminals are almost as imaginative as examiners when it comes to inflicting harm, so you need to take this stuff seriously.

Cyber Security is important to People and Organisations

1) Cyber security aims to protect networks, data, programs and computers against damage, cyber attacks and unauthorised access. It covers the technologies (e.g. anti-malware software), practices (e.g. network policies) and processes (e.g. penetration testing) used to do this.

2) Cyber attacks can target individuals, organisations or even governments. Hackers (see p77) often target organisations with the aim of accessing lots of sensitive information at once. There have been cases of millions of people's bank details being compromised by attacks on a single organisation.

Cyber attacks against governments or militaries, are sometimes called cyber warfare.

Malware is software that can harm devices

1) Malware (malicious software) is code that is designed to cause harm or gain unauthorised access to a computer system. It is often installed on someone's device without their knowledge or consent.

2) There are several different ways that malware can get onto a device — for example, being downloaded in an email attachment or hidden on removable media (e.g. USB drive or SD card).

3) Typical actions of malware include:

- Deleting or modifying files.
- Locking files — ransomware encrypts all the files on a computer. The user receives a message demanding a large sum of money be paid in exchange for a decryption key.
- Displaying unwanted adverts — adware can cause pop-up ads that cannot be closed.
- Monitoring the user — spyware secretly tracks actions like key presses and sends info to the hacker, who might be able to work out things like passwords and bank details.
- Altering permissions — rootkits can give hackers administrator-level access to devices.

4) Malware can spread between devices in different ways.

- Viruses attach (by copying themselves) to certain files, e.g. .exe files and autorun scripts. Users spread them by copying infected files and activate them by opening infected files.
- Worms are like viruses but they self-replicate without any user help, meaning they can spread very quickly. They exploit weaknesses in network security.
- Trojans are malware disguised as legitimate software. Unlike viruses and worms, trojans don't replicate themselves — users install them not realising they have a hidden purpose.

Malware can also be used to carry out Pharming

1) Pharming is where a user is directed to a fake version of a website (like a banking or shopping site), that looks just like the real thing, with the aim that the user won't notice the difference.

2) When the user inputs their personal information into the website, they're actually handing it all over to the criminals, who can then access their genuine account.

3) Pharming is often carried out using malware that automatically redirects people from legitimate sites to fake ones. Ensuring that anti-malware software is up-to-date can reduce the risk of these attacks.

4) Internet browsers can use web filters to prevent users from accessing these fake sites.

Jay suspected that this could be a farming website...

A worm got into my computer — I shouldn't leave it on the lawn...

You don't need to know every single type of malware out there, but learning all of the examples here will give you a great overview of how malware gets in and the chaos it can wreak once it's there.

Cyber Security Threats

Sci-fi movies might have lead you to believe that breaking into a network is all about tapping on a keyboard really quickly, but you'd be surprised how often it's done the old-fashioned way — manipulating people.

People are often the Weak Point in secure systems

Social engineering is a way of gaining sensitive information or illegal access to networks by influencing people, usually the employees of large companies. Social engineering comes in many different forms:

PHISHING

1) Phishing is when criminals send emails or texts to people claiming to be from a well-known business, e.g. a bank. The emails often lead the victim to a fake website, just like pharming.

2) Phishing emails are often sent to thousands of people, in the hope that someone will read the email and believe its content is legitimate.

3) Many email programs, browsers and firewalls have anti-phishing features that will reduce the number of phishing emails received. There are often signs that you can spot, like typos. Emails asking users to follow links or update personal details should be treated with caution.

SHOULDERING

1) Shouldering or shoulder surfing is watching and observing a person's activity (typically over their shoulder).

2) Some examples of this are spying someone's PIN number at a cash machine, or watching someone putting their password into a secured computer.

3) It doesn't require any technical expertise or any planning. It's simple, but it can work. You can reduce risk by being discreet, e.g. covering the keypad when you enter your PIN.

> That's right, type away...

> Input my password? If you say so...

BLAGGING

1) Blagging or pretexting is when someone makes up a story or pretends to be someone they're not, to persuade the victim to share information or do things they wouldn't normally do.

2) For example, a potential attacker could email someone, pretending to be one of their friends, saying they are stuck in a foreign country and need them to send money.

3) Another common method is to phone the victim, trying to gain their trust by persuading them that they are someone important — e.g. their boss's boss.

4) Criminals that use these tactics often try to pressure people, or rush them into giving away details without giving it proper thought. One way to reduce risk is to use security measures that can't be given away, e.g. biometrics (see p72).

Penetration Testing can Test a system's Cyber Security

1) Penetration testing (or pentesting) is when organisations employ specialists to simulate potential attacks to their system. It's used to identify possible weaknesses in their cyber security. The results of the test are then reported back so that vulnerabilities can be fixed.

2) There are two different forms of penetration test — white box and black box.

- White box penetration testing simulates a malicious insider who has knowledge of the current system, e.g. an employee at the organisation. The person carrying out the test will be given user credentials to see what they can do with them.

- Black box penetration testing simulates an external cyber attack. The person carrying out the test will not be given any credentials, but will try to hack the organisation in any way they can.

The builders throw parties in the name of social engineering...

The best way to prevent social engineering in the workplace is to make employees aware of the dangers — sometimes pentesters will use social engineering tactics so that employees gain experience dealing with them. Don't give away any details unless you're absolutely sure of who you're giving them to. Now excuse me, Derek has emailed saying that he needs me to send him £5000 to get home from Ibiza...

Cyber Security Threats

Most organisations have a <u>network policy</u> — a set of rules and procedures that the organisation will follow to ensure their network is protected against any possible security threats, e.g. a cyber attack.

Networks need to be Protected against Threats

Organisations must keep their <u>networks secure</u> from <u>hackers</u> in order to protect sensitive information and comply with <u>data protection laws</u> (see p77). They can use several methods to help them do this:

Encryption is when data is translated into a code which only someone with the <u>correct key</u> can access, meaning unauthorised users cannot read it. Encrypted text is called <u>cipher text</u>, whereas data which has not been encrypted is called <u>plain text</u>. Encryption is essential for sending data over a network <u>securely</u>.

This book is encrypted.
The key is to stop reading it upside down.

Shut up malware!
Captain Firewall to the rescue!

Anti-malware software is designed to find and stop <u>malware</u> from damaging a network and the devices on it. There are <u>different types</u> of anti-malware software, e.g. <u>virus scanners</u> (p59).

Firewalls examine <u>all data</u> entering and leaving a network, <u>identify potential threats</u> using a set of <u>security rules</u> and <u>block</u> any unwanted data. Firewalls can be <u>software</u> or <u>hardware</u> — often <u>both</u> types are used for <u>extra security</u>.

Automatic software updates are used to <u>patch</u> (fix) any identified <u>security holes</u> in a piece of software. Software that is unpatched or outdated could be more easily <u>exploited</u> by hackers, malware and viruses.

User access levels control which parts of the network different groups of users can access. E.g. <u>business managers</u> are likely to have a <u>higher access level</u> allowing them to access <u>more sensitive data</u>, like pay information. User access levels <u>limit</u> the number of people with access to important data, so help to prevent attacks from <u>within</u> the organisation.

MAC address filtering is a way of making sure the only people on a <u>network</u> are <u>trusted users</u>. It checks the <u>unique identification</u> (MAC address) of each device that tries to connect to the network and only lets <u>allowed devices</u> join the network.

MAC addresses are unique identifiers assigned to network devices by the manufacturer — they can't be changed.

Authentication confirms your Identity

<u>User authentication</u> exists to make sure that <u>anyone</u> trying to access a network or use a system is who they say they are. This <u>prevents unauthorised people</u> from accessing data from the network.

Enter Password
Chihuahua — ✗ Too Weak
Please Enter a <u>Stronger</u> Password
Rottweil

Passwords are a <u>simple</u> method of checking someone's identity. They should be strong — many characters long, use a <u>combination</u> of letters, numbers and symbols, and be <u>changed regularly</u>. Weak or default passwords are a big security risk.

Biometric measures use <u>scanners</u> to identify people by a unique part of their <u>body</u>, e.g. <u>fingerprint</u>, <u>retina</u>, etc. They have many different uses — for example, many <u>smartphones</u> now contain fingerprint scanners to <u>prevent unauthorised access</u>.

Email confirmation is used by most web services that require <u>account registration</u> to confirm that the <u>email address</u> belongs to the person registering. It is also used to stop people from using <u>fake</u> email addresses to <u>sign up</u> for things.

CAPTCHA stands for 'Completely Automated Public Turing test to tell Computers and Humans Apart' and is designed to <u>prevent programs</u> from <u>automatically</u> doing certain things, like <u>creating user accounts</u> on a website. It usually consists of a <u>simple task</u>, like typing out a <u>blurred</u> and <u>distorted word</u> from an image, or <u>recognising</u> things like animals and signposts.

CAPTCHA

Learn this page and your exam grade should be fairly secure...

You could be asked about threats or prevention, so make sure you know the last three pages really well. Heed Captain Firewall's wise words, ~~'die malware, just DIE!!!'~~ I mean 'preparation is key to success'.

Revision Questions for Section Six

From passwords to packets to PANs to protocols... you should now know petworks pinside pout.

- Try these questions and <u>tick off each one</u> when you <u>get it right</u>.
- When you've done <u>all the questions</u> for a topic and are <u>completely happy</u> with it, tick off the topic.

<u>Networks, Hardware and Topologies (p65-67)</u> ☑

1) What's the difference between a LAN and a WAN?
2) What type of network is Bluetooth® used for?
3) Give five benefits and four drawbacks of using a network.
4) What are the following devices used for?   a) NICs   b) switches   c) routers
5) Describe three different types of network cable.
6) What type of network is commonly referred to as 'Wi-Fi®'?
7) Give two benefits and two drawbacks of using wireless networks over wired.
8) Give two advantages and two disadvantages of using a star network topology.
9) Describe the key features of a bus network topology.

<u>Network Protocols (p68-69)</u> ☑

10) What is the definition of a protocol?
11) List the 4 layers of the TCP/IP protocol model and the 4 layers of the ultimate cake.
12) Give three reasons why we divide protocols into layers.
13) What does each of the following stand for? Describe in a sentence what each one does:
        HTTP   HTTPS   FTP   IMAP   SMTP
14) Explain the differences between how TCP and UDP work.
15) Give one example of when you would use TCP, and one example of when you would use UDP.
16) Briefly describe how packet switching works.
17) Explain the difference between Wi-Fi® bands and Wi-Fi® channels.
18) What does WPA™ stand for and what does it do?
19) Name the family of protocols in charge of transmitting data over wired LANs.

<u>Cyber Security Threats (p70-72)</u> ☑

20) Give three reasons why someone might carry out a cyber attack.
21) List five malicious actions that malicious software might maliciously carry out.
22) Describe three ways that malware can spread between devices.
23) What is pharming?
24) What is meant by social engineering?
25) Give three social engineering methods, and say how you could reduce the risk of each.
26) Explain the difference between white box and black box penetration testing.
27) Briefly describe six ways of protecting networks against threats.
28) What is user authentication?
29) Give three precautions you should take with your passwords.
30) My smartphone has a fingerprint scanner. What is the name for this kind of security measure?
31) Write down the two words in the image below. What kind of test is this and what does it prove?

fabric investigate

Ethical Issues

Despite what you might think, computer science doesn't just exist in a well-ventilated bubble — it affects all of our lives. Computers, smartphones and other new technologies impact different people in different ways.

Issues created by technology come in Different Flavours

1) <u>Ethical</u> issues are about what would be considered <u>right</u> and <u>wrong</u> by society.
2) <u>Legal</u> issues are about what's actually <u>right</u> and <u>wrong</u> in the eyes of <u>the law</u>.
3) <u>Environmental</u> issues are about how we impact the natural world.

There is often <u>overlap</u> between ethical, legal and environmental issues.

> Exam questions on issues could cover topics from earlier sections too, e.g. cloud storage (p56), wireless networks (p66) and cyber security (p70-72).

Digital Technology raises many Ethical Issues

As new digital technology becomes available, it can create a whole bunch of ethical issues.

1) <u>Smartphones</u> have allowed us to keep in touch much more easily, but have also allowed people to <u>neglect face-to-face interaction</u>. Some might say that it is making people <u>more rude</u> and <u>less sociable</u>.

2) <u>Wearable technology</u> has <u>many positive effects</u> — for example, <u>wireless headsets</u> may stop people from using their phone while driving and <u>fitness trackers</u> can help to promote healthy lifestyles. However, it can also cause problems. <u>Smart glasses</u> with built-in cameras have sparked controversy — people say the fact that they could be used to secretly photograph people is an <u>invasion of privacy</u>.

3) <u>Computer-based implants</u> (chips that are surgically inserted into the body) may become more common in the future. They could allow better monitoring of our <u>health</u> and might make our daily lives more <u>convenient</u>, but will likely be <u>expensive</u> and may lead to <u>less privacy</u>.

4) <u>Autonomous vehicles</u> aim to <u>automate</u> the process of driving by doing <u>some or all</u> of the <u>work of the driver</u>. Many modern cars are <u>partially autonomous</u>, but some companies are developing fully <u>self-driving cars</u>. With no need for a human driver, car journeys could become <u>more accessible</u> to non-drivers. By <u>communicating</u> with other vehicles and <u>removing human error</u>, they could also be <u>safer</u> and <u>improve traffic flow</u>.

5) However, self-driving cars should be able to cope with unpredictable <u>human drivers</u> and <u>pedestrians</u>, which current technology can't do yet. There is a risk that they could be <u>hacked</u>, raising questions about who is <u>responsible</u> in a crash.

> Going for a drive, see you later human!

6) There are also more complicated <u>dilemmas</u>, such as whether they should be programmed to <u>prioritise</u> some lives over others when a <u>fatal collision</u> is inevitable, and whether <u>programmers</u> should be expected to make those sorts of <u>decisions</u>.

Unequal access to technology has caused a Digital Divide

1) Some people have <u>greater access</u> than others to these new digital technologies. People who have limited access to technology are at a heavy <u>disadvantage</u> — this is referred to as the <u>digital divide</u>.

CAUSES OF THE DIGITAL DIVIDE
- Some people don't have enough <u>money</u> to buy new devices like <u>smartphones</u> and <u>laptops</u>.
- <u>Urban</u> areas may have better <u>network coverage</u> than <u>rural</u> areas.
- Some people <u>don't know how</u> to use the Internet and other new technologies, and so are shut out of the opportunities they offer. This is a problem for many <u>older people</u> who haven't grown up with computers and so have little experience with them.

2) The <u>global divide</u> is created by the fact that the level of access to technology is different in different <u>countries</u>. People in richer countries tend to have greater access to technology than people in poorer countries. The Internet and other technologies have created lots of opportunities for the people with access to them, so this has <u>increased</u> the inequality between poorer and richer countries.

If you've got an issue, here's a high-tech nose-blowing device...

Exam questions may ask you to talk about ethical, legal <u>and</u> environmental issues, rather than just one. The more points you can make, the better — just make sure all your points are relevant to the question.

Ethical Issues

Computers have had a tremendous impact on society — it's difficult to imagine some of the things we do today without them. Just remember that this technological revolution is not always smiles and rainbows...

Probably the most issue-ful technology is *The Internet*

1) The Internet gives people greater anonymity, which can enable anti-social and abusive behaviour:
   - Cyberbullying is when somebody uses the Internet to deliberately intimidate, insult or humiliate someone. It can cause serious distress — people have been driven to suicide because of these attacks.
   - Trolling is when somebody tries to cause public arguments with others online, only making comments which frustrate other people. Trolls normally do this for their own amusement or to gain attention.

2) People now use the Internet for things they'd traditionally do in person, e.g. online banking and shopping. This means that organisations now store a lot of our personal data — they have an ethical (and legal) responsibility to have good cyber security (see p70) to prevent things like identity theft.

3) This is also true of companies providing the public with wireless access to the Internet (e.g. cafes that offer free Wi-Fi®). Many would argue that they also have a responsibility to restrict access to certain websites (such as gambling and pornography sites), as children could be able to gain access.

4) The ability to stream music and television online has allowed customers to access media conveniently and cheaply, either for free or through a subscription service. But users of these services often don't own what they're paying for, and they can lose access if their subscription ends or if the service closes down.

5) There are also many online services that are now offered for free — cloud storage (p56) and webmail are examples of this. Often, these services will have limits on what you can access for free, and a superior 'premium' service that costs money. This could help to reduce the digital divide by providing partial services to people who otherwise couldn't afford them.

6) This type of business model can also be seen in mobile games — however, some say that these games exploit people with more impulsive spending habits. There have also been cases of parents accidentally allowing their children to spend hundreds of pounds on these games.

Technology is also changing *How Businesses Operate*

1) A lot of businesses expect people to be able to use technology and access services online. For example, employers may expect people to be able to apply for jobs online, and many require employees to have at least some basic computer skills. However, some people may not have access to technology for various reasons (see p74), which puts them at an unfair disadvantage.

2) The popularity of mobile devices has lead to some businesses insisting that employees carry a smartphone with them all the time, so that they can always be contacted, either by phone or by email. This can be stressful for employees who feel they can never really switch off from work.

3) In fact, some companies have taken this one step further and offered their employees computer chip implants that can open security doors and access their computer. This is more secure than password or keycard systems, but many people find the idea of implanting technology in humans to be unethical.

4) Marketing and advertising have also been greatly affected by new technology. Pop-ups appear all over the Internet and targeted adverts are shown to people on social media sites. This has led to people feeling swamped by advertising online, and has made programs like AdBlock popular. However, lots of free services are funded by advertising money, so if everybody blocked the adverts, then the providers of these services would lose their income and may have to start charging for the service instead.

5) Even though businesses can take advantage of technology in lots of ways, they have to be careful — if they ignored the ethical impact of their actions, even if they were legal, they could lose public trust. Many businesses have a code of conduct (a set of rules that the business and its employees will follow) to show the public that they take these ethical issues seriously.

Don't mind grumpy over there — he's got a chip in his shoulder...

I'm out of breath trying to keep up with all this new technology... Anyway, just remember that businesses are big users and developers of technology, but they don't always have everyone's best interests at heart.

Ethical Issues

It's quite concerning to think how many people actually saw your last social media status. Guess we should count ourselves lucky though — some people in the world don't get to access social media at all.

It's hard to keep information *Private* on the Internet

1) Most people generally want to be able to keep their personal information <u>private</u>. However, this rarely happens in practice, as many online services require you to provide your details in order to use them. For example:

   • Many websites (shopping, banking, etc.) require users to provide <u>personal information</u> in order to set up an account, e.g. date of birth and address.

   • <u>Social media</u> websites actively <u>encourage</u> you to post even more personal information, including photographs and details of your job and social life.

2) Users will accept a <u>privacy agreement</u> before using many websites and software. The trouble is that very few people actually read these, so most are <u>unaware</u> of what they're agreeing to. Even if they <u>do</u> read the terms, users often have <u>no choice</u> but to agree if they want to use the website or software at all.

3) Companies can do lots of things with your details as long as they stay <u>within the bounds</u> of the privacy agreement. They can make your information available to <u>other people</u>, or <u>sell</u> your <u>personal details</u>, <u>buying habits</u> etc. to other organisations (who could use it to send you <u>targeted adverts</u> or <u>spam</u> emails).

4) Users can take steps to make the information they share more <u>private</u>, e.g. change their <u>privacy settings</u> on social media sites (which are often fairly relaxed by <u>default</u>).

5) Users have to trust companies to keep their data <u>secure</u>. But this doesn't always happen — there have been various <u>high profile cases</u> where customer data held by large companies has been <u>leaked</u> or <u>stolen</u>.

Surveillance *and* Censorship *are controversial issues*

1) <u>Computer surveillance</u> is when someone <u>monitors</u> what other people are accessing on the Internet.

2) Many countries use some form of surveillance. Government <u>security services</u> may use packet sniffers and other software to <u>monitor Internet traffic</u>, looking out for certain <u>key words</u> or <u>phrases</u> that might alert them to illegal activities, terrorism, etc. Often, governments will push for <u>greater powers</u> (e.g. access to private emails) to assist in catching criminals, but might face <u>opposition</u> from the public.

3) In some countries, <u>Internet Service Providers</u> (ISPs) <u>keep records</u> of all websites visited by all its customers for a certain amount of time, and may be <u>legally required</u> to share data with <u>security services</u>.

4) <u>Internet censorship</u> is when someone tries to <u>control</u> what other people can access on the Internet. Governments use censorship to restrict access to certain <u>information</u>.

5) Some countries have very <u>strict</u> censorship, where they <u>restrict access</u> to websites such as Facebook®, YouTube™ and Twitter, or websites that are <u>critical</u> of the government. In other countries, citizens can only access the Internet from government-controlled <u>access points</u>.

Not too sure about this new censorship policy.

6) Many governments use <u>some form</u> of censorship. Many countries (including the UK) restrict access to pornography, gambling and other inappropriate websites in order to <u>protect children</u>.

7) Censorship and surveillance are <u>controversial</u> topics. Some people support them in some form, e.g. to protect children or to stop terrorism. Others are completely against them and will often campaign against what they call <u>cyber censorship</u> and <u>mass surveillance</u>.

---

* This content has been removed to protect you from bad jokes... *

Do you ever get the feeling you're being watched? No? Just me then. The weird thing about the stuff on this page is that everyone knows it's happening but no-one does anything about it — the Internet is such a big part of modern life that for many people their loss of privacy is a price worth paying. Other people aren't so keen about losing their privacy though, which I guess is why these issues are so controversial.

Legal Issues

Since computers went mainstream, the law has had to keep up with the way people use and abuse them. The Internet causes lots of issues, since it's so difficult to police what people do online.

Laws Control the use of your Personal Data

1) When an organisation stores someone's personal data on their system, that person is entitled to certain <u>rights</u>, stated in <u>data protection laws</u>. These rights can be summarised by the <u>principles</u> shown here.

2) Before collecting personal data, an organisation must <u>register</u> with the government, saying <u>what data</u> they'll collect, and <u>how</u> they'll use it.

3) It is the <u>responsibility</u> of the <u>organisation</u> to make sure that they follow the <u>rules</u> — if not, they could face <u>large fines</u>.

4) Organisations have a <u>legal obligation</u> to have good <u>cyber security</u> (p70) on their networks to keep personal data secure. This can be hard for <u>small businesses</u>, who may not be able to afford top-of-the-range <u>security software</u>.

5) Companies using <u>cloud storage</u> (see p56) to store personal data must ensure that the service is <u>trustworthy</u> and <u>reliable</u>.

Data Protection Principles

- Data must only be used in a fair, lawful and transparent way.
- Data must only be used for the specified purpose.
- Data should be kept safe and secure.
- Data should not be kept longer than is necessary.
- Data should be adequate, relevant and not excessive for the specified use.
- Data must be accurate and kept up to date.

The Computer Misuse Act prevents illegal access to files

The <u>Computer Misuse Act</u> was introduced to stop <u>hacking</u> and <u>cyber crime</u> (see below). It introduced <u>three new offences</u>:

How do you like my new smartwatch?

The long arm of the law.

1) Gaining <u>unauthorised access</u> to a private network or device, e.g. through <u>hacking</u> (just accessing a network could get you a fine or prison sentence).

2) Gaining <u>unauthorised access</u> to a network or device <u>in order to commit a crime</u>, like stealing data or destroying the network.

3) <u>Unauthorised modification of computer material</u> — e.g. deleting or changing files. The Act also makes it illegal to <u>make</u>, <u>supply</u> or <u>obtain malware</u>.

Cyber Crime is a major problem

1) <u>Cyber crime</u> refers to any <u>illegal</u> activity that involves <u>computers</u>. The most infamous type of cyber criminal are <u>hackers</u>.

> <u>Hacking</u> refers to <u>gaining access</u> to a system by <u>exploiting weaknesses</u> in its security. This is usually done to <u>steal</u> or <u>destroy data</u>, or to <u>infect</u> the system with <u>malware</u> (p70). However, some companies employ 'good' hackers to <u>identify vulnerabilities</u> through <u>penetration testing</u> (p71).

2) There are lots of <u>different methods</u> that hackers use to <u>attack systems</u>, including:
- <u>passive</u> attacks — <u>monitoring</u> data on a network, e.g. using <u>packet sniffer</u> software.
- <u>active</u> attacks — using <u>malware</u> or other means to attack a system <u>directly</u>.
- <u>brute force</u> attacks — using <u>automated software</u> and <u>trial-and-error</u> to crack <u>passwords</u>.
- <u>denial-of-service</u> attacks — <u>preventing</u> people from using a network by <u>flooding</u> it with <u>useless traffic</u>.

3) Since cyber criminals tend to have a <u>good understanding</u> of networks and security measures, they often know how to <u>avoid</u> being tracked down, making it <u>very difficult</u> to <u>catch</u> and <u>prosecute</u> them.

Hacking is computer misuse, so stop chopping up your laptop...

Make sure that you understand what hacking is all about (that's not an invitation to try it out, though). You don't need to memorise all of the data protection principles given above, but the more you know about it, the more points you'll be able to make in the exam. And that's why we're here, right?

Environmental Issues

Devices have a huge environmental impact. Take a smartphone — it's made of materials that have to be mined from the Earth, when it's used it consumes energy, and when it's thrown away it could end up on a landfill site.

When we *Make* devices we use up *Natural Resources*

1) Electronic devices contain lots of <u>raw materials</u>.

2) <u>Plastics</u> (which are used for casing and other parts) come from <u>crude oil</u>.

3) Devices also contain many <u>precious metals</u> like gold, silver, copper, mercury, palladium, platinum, indium and fancyshinyinium*. Many of these metals only occur naturally in <u>tiny quantities</u>.

4) Extracting these materials uses lots of <u>energy</u>, creates <u>pollution</u> and depletes scarce <u>natural resources</u>.

When we *Use* devices we use *Energy... lots of it*

All the billions of devices in the world today are consuming energy in the form of <u>electricity</u> — a lot of it.

1) Most electricity is made using <u>non-renewable</u> resources like coal, oil and gas. <u>Extracting</u> these resources and <u>producing electricity</u> in power stations causes lots of <u>pollution</u> including greenhouse gases.

One for me and one for you.

2) All computers generate <u>heat</u> and require cooling. The powerful <u>servers</u> used by businesses and the Internet are a particular problem. They're very <u>power hungry</u> and require special <u>air-conditioned</u> rooms to keep them cool. That means using even more energy and more pollution.

3) Devices also <u>waste</u> a lot of energy. Servers normally only use a <u>small proportion</u> of their <u>processing power</u>. People often leave their desktops, laptops and smartphones <u>idle</u>. This means these devices are using a lot of energy without actually doing <u>anything</u>.

4) There are several ways to <u>reduce</u> the amount of energy wasted by devices:

- <u>Virtual servers</u> are <u>software-based</u> servers rather than real machines. Multiple virtual servers can run on one physical server, so the physical server can run at <u>full capacity</u>.

- <u>Switching off</u> mobile devices <u>overnight</u>, or putting them into <u>sleep</u> mode, can save power.

- Devices often use more energy when searching for a <u>wireless</u> connection. Disabling this, or using a <u>wired</u> connection, could preserve battery life.

When we *Throw Away* devices we create loads of *E-waste*

1) <u>E-waste</u> is a huge problem — the world creates <u>20-50 million tonnes</u> of e-waste every year. Modern devices have a very <u>short life</u> before they're discarded — either because they <u>break</u> or because people want to <u>upgrade</u> (particularly with smartphones).

2) <u>Device manufacturers</u> and <u>retailers</u> can contribute to this problem. The latest <u>mobile devices</u> can provide <u>convenient</u> and <u>exciting features</u> for customers, but this can encourage users to <u>replace</u> their devices <u>more frequently</u>, which creates lots of e-waste. Short <u>warranties</u> (e.g. 1 year) can also make <u>replacing</u> or <u>upgrading</u> a device a better option than <u>repairing</u> it.

3) The Waste Electric and Electronic Equipment (<u>WEEE</u>) directive was created to tackle the e-waste problem. The WEEE has rules for disposing of e-waste <u>safely</u>, to promote <u>reuse</u> (e.g. refurbishing broken devices to use again) and <u>recycling</u> (e.g. extracting the devices' <u>precious metals</u>).

4) To <u>cut costs</u>, a lot of e-waste is sent to certain African and Asian countries which have less strict regulations. Here, most of it ends up in <u>landfill</u> and can be a hazard — toxic chemicals can leak into the <u>ground water</u> and harm wildlife.

Don't (e-)waste your time — use your energy to learn this page...

I know this sounds very negative, but it's not all bad news — the Internet lets us talk to each other without having to travel long distances in pollution-spouting vehicles, cloud storage has reduced the need for things like CDs, and wireless networking means fewer resources are wasted on cables. *OK, that one may be made up...

Revision Questions for Section Seven

Well, that section had a lot of issues — thankfully you're not here to solve its problems, just learn its content.

- Try these questions and <u>tick off each one</u> when you <u>get it right</u>.
- When you've done <u>all the questions</u> for a topic and are <u>completely happy</u> with it, tick off the topic.

<u>Ethical Issues (p74-76)</u> ☑

1) Define each type of issue in a sentence:
   a) ethical   b) legal   c) environmental ☑

2) Give one positive and one negative ethical issue caused by:
   a) mobile devices   b) wearable technology   c) computer-based implants ☑

3) What are autonomous vehicles and why could they be beneficial? ☑

4) Suggest a negative ethical issue associated with autonomous vehicles. ☑

5) Give three reasons why a digital divide exists. ☑

6) What is: a) cyberbullying?   b) trolling? ☑

7) Give a reason why cyberbullying and trolling have become so common. ☑

8) Give two examples of services that have been changed by new technology. ☑

9) Explain, in 30 words or less, how businesses can be affected by each of the following:
   a) mobile devices   b) the Internet   c) computer-based implants ☑

10) Give two reasons why someone might give their personal details to a website. ☑

11) Give two problems with many online companies' privacy agreements. ☑

12) What can you do to make the information you share online more private? ☑

13) Explain the difference between censorship and surveillance. ☑

14) Give one argument for and one against Internet censorship. ☑

15) Give one argument for and one against governments carrying out Internet surveillance. ☑

<u>Legal Issues (p77)</u> ☑

16) a) When do data protection laws apply?
    b) Give three data protection principles. ☑

17) What could happen to an organisation if they don't follow the data protection laws? ☑

18) What three offences does the Computer Misuse Act cover? ☑

19) a) What is a hacker?
    b) Describe four methods that a hacker might use to attack a system. ☑

<u>Environmental Issues (p78)</u> ☑

20) Give three examples of natural resources which are used to make computers. ☑

21) Explain how a device's need for energy impacts the environment. ☑

22) Give three ways to reduce the amount of energy devices waste. ☑

23) What is e-waste and why do we generate a lot of it? ☑

24) Describe an environmental danger caused by e-waste left in landfill sites. ☑

Answers

Page 7 — Section One

Q8 E.g.

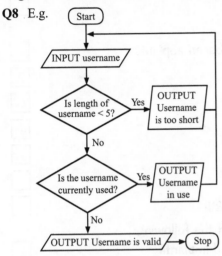

Q11 a) <u>Binary Search</u>:
The middle item is the 4th item, *Dagenham,* which comes before *Morpeth*.
So <u>lose first half of list</u> to leave:
Morpeth, Usk, Watford
The middle item of the new list is the 2nd item, *Usk*, which comes after *Morpeth* so <u>lose second half of list</u> to leave: *Morpeth*
The middle item of the new list is the 1st item, which is *Morpeth*, so you've found the correct item.

<small>Even when there is one entry left you still have to carry on with the algorithm to check that it is the correct entry.</small>

b) <u>Linear Search</u>:
Ashington ≠ Morpeth
Brecon ≠ Morpeth
Chester ≠ Morpeth
Dagenham ≠ Morpeth
Morpeth = Morpeth
You've found the correct item.

Q13 b) **1st pass (4 swaps):**
<u>O, B</u>, A, P, G, L
B, <u>O, A</u>, P, G, L
B, A, O, <u>P, G</u>, L
B, A, O, G, <u>P, L</u>
B, A, O, G, L, P
2nd pass (3 swaps):
<u>B, A</u>, O, G, L, P
A, B, <u>O, G</u>, L, P
A, B, G, <u>O, L</u>, P
A, B, G, L, O, P
3rd pass (no swaps):
A, B, G, L, O, P

Q15 a)

8	7	5	1	3	6	4	2

| 8 | 7 | 5 | 1 | | 3 | 6 | 4 | 2 |

| 8 | 7 | 5 | 1 | | 3 | 6 | | 4 | 2 |

| 8 | 7 | | 5 | 1 | | 3 | 6 | | 4 | 2 |

| 7 | 8 | | 1 | 5 | | 3 | 6 | | 2 | 4 |

| 1 | 5 | 7 | 8 | | 2 | 3 | 4 | 6 |

| 1 | 2 | 3 | 4 | 5 | 6 | 7 | 8 |

b) **1st pass (4 swaps):**
8 7 5 1 <u>3</u> 6 4 2
8 7 5 3 <u>1</u> 6 4 2
8 7 5 3 6 <u>1</u> 4 2
8 7 5 3 6 4 <u>1</u> 2
8 7 5 3 6 4 2 1
2nd pass (2 swaps):
8 7 5 <u>3</u> 6 4 2 1
8 7 5 6 <u>3</u> 4 2 1
8 7 5 6 4 3 2 1
3rd pass (1 swap):
8 7 <u>5</u> 6 4 3 2 1
8 7 6 5 4 3 2 1
4th pass (no swaps):
8 7 6 5 4 3 2 1

Page 28 — Section Two

Q2 a) STRING_TO_INT('1234')
b) REAL_TO_STRING(0.578)
c) INT_TO_STRING(8)
d) STRING_TO_REAL('0.75')

Q5 b) (i) 7
(ii) 2
(iii) 'mage'

Q9
```
first_day ← USERINPUT
IF first_day = 'Sunday'
OR first_day = 'Monday' THEN
    OUTPUT 5
ELSE
    OUTPUT 4
ENDIF
```

Q10
```
FOR i ← 1 TO 100
    roll ← RANDOM_INT(1, 8)
    OUTPUT roll
ENDFOR
```

Q12 a) OUTPUT chars[4]
b) chars[2] ← 'D'
c)
```
FOR i ← 0 to 9
    chars[i] ← 'N'
ENDFOR
```

Q13
```
FOR i ← 0 TO 9
    FOR j ← 0 TO 9
        multiply[i][j] ← i * j
    ENDFOR
ENDFOR
```

Answers

Q22 def printTenFor(string1):
    for i in range(10):
        print(string1)

    def printTenWhile(string2):
      n = 1
      while n <= 10:
        print(string2)
        n = n + 1

Page 33 — Section Three

Q9 Range check — the program checks if the user has entered a year between 1900 and 2016 before breaking out of the REPEAT-UNTIL loop.

Q12 On the 4th line of code the variable age is an integer so it cannot be concatenated with a string. Instead of using the age variable, the ageString variable should be used.
The code doesn't do anything if the age is exactly 16.
Either change the first condition to age >= 16
or the second condition to age <= 16.

Q14 For example:
- Normal input data (e.g. 'art')
- No input (e.g. ' ')
- A string with no anagram (e.g. 'x')
- Mixed case string (e.g. 'aRT')
- Other characters (e.g. 2?#)

Q16

x	arr[x]	total
		1
0	2	2
1	5	10
2	1	10
3	2	20
4	3	60

Page 49 — Section Four

Q2 (A OR B) AND C
or in symbols: (A + B) . C

A	B	C	A OR B	(A OR B) AND C
0	0	0	0	0
0	0	1	0	0
0	1	0	1	0
0	1	1	1	1
1	0	0	1	0
1	0	1	1	1
1	1	0	1	0
1	1	1	1	1

Q5 a) 0.2 gigabytes
    b) 1 600 000 000 bits

Q6 10001111

Q8 a) (i) 10001
      (ii) 10010100
      (iii) 11110000
    b) (i) 11
      (ii) 94
      (iii) F0

Q9 a) (i) 56
      (ii) 159
      (iii) 43
    b) (i) 38
      (ii) 9F
      (iii) 2B

Q10 a) (i) 74
      (ii) 117
      (iii) 217
    b) (i) 1001010
      (ii) 1110101
      (iii) 11011001

Q22 a) (4, P), (2, Q), (3, R),
      (6, S), (5, P), (3, Q)

b)

Character	Huffman Code
P	0
Q	111
R	110
S	10

c) (i) $23 \times 7 = 161$ bits.
   (ii) The number of bits needed for each character using the Huffman coding is shown in the table below:

Character	Code	Frequency	Bits Needed
P	0	9	$1 \times 9 = 9$
Q	111	5	$3 \times 5 = 15$
R	110	3	$3 \times 3 = 9$
S	10	6	$2 \times 6 = 12$

This gives a total of:
$9 + 15 + 9 + 12 = 45$ bits.
   (iii) $8 \times 2 \times 6 = 96$ bits

Page 64 — Section Five

Q29 The query will return the name field of any records in the staff table that have a salary field value greater than or equal to 35 000. The returned names will be ordered based on their salary field values from low to high.

Glossary and Index

A

abstraction Picking out the important bits of information. **1**

active attack A network attack where the hacker attempts to change data or introduce malware. **77**

adware A type of malware which displays unwanted pop-up advertisements on a computer. **70**

algorithm A step-by-step set of rules or instructions. **1-6**

algorithmic thinking Coming up with an algorithm to solve a problem. **1**

alphanumeric The collective name for letters, digits and symbols. **11, 43**

analogue signal A continuous signal which can't be processed by a computer. **45**

AND One of the Boolean operators.
  logic gate **34-36**
  operator **16**
  symbol **36**

anti-malware software Software designed to stop malware from damaging a computer or network. **72**

application A piece of software written to help users do various tasks, often through a graphical user interface with menus and toolbars. **50, 57**

application layer One of the layers in the TCP/IP network protocol model. **68**

architecture Describes how the CPU works and interacts with the other parts of the computer system. **52**

argument A value that a parameter of a subroutine actually takes. **21**

arithmetic logic unit (ALU) The part of the CPU that carries out arithmetic and Boolean operations. **51, 52**

arithmetic operator An operator that programs use to carry out simple mathematical operations. **9**
  in Python® **24**

array A data structure where data values of the same type are stored and defined under one variable name. **18, 19**
  one-dimensional **18**
  two-dimensional **19**

ASCII A 7-bit (or 8-bit) character set consisting of 128 characters. **43**

assembler A program that turns assembly language into machine code. **60**

assembly language A low-level language. **60**

assignment operator (←) Assigns the value on the right hand side to the name on the left hand side. **9**
  in Python® **24**

authentication A process for checking the identity of the user. **30**

automatic software updates A method of keeping software up-to-date so that any security holes can be removed. **72**

autonomous vehicles Vehicles that perform some or all of the work of the driver. **74**

B

backup utility A type of utility program that creates a copy of a system's files and settings to be restored in the event of data loss. **59**

bandwidth The amount of data that can be transferred on a network in a given time. **66**

binary A counting system using base-2 consisting of 0s and 1s. **38-40**
  addition **39**
  converting to/from decimal **38**
  converting to/from hexadecimal **42**

binary search algorithm **4**

binary shift Moving the bits in a binary number left or right and filling the gaps with 0s. **40**

biometric measures Ways of authenticating someone's identity using unique parts of their body, such as fingerprints or retinas. **72**

BIOS (Basic Input Output System) Software stored in ROM responsible for booting up a computer system. **53**

bit A binary digit, either 0 or 1. **37**

bitmap image A graphic that is made up of pixels. **44**

bit rate The number of bits used per second of sampled audio. **45**

black box penetration testing A form of penetration testing where the tester is not given any system credentials. Used to simulate an external cyber attack. **71**

blagging Using an invented scenario to persuade someone to share information, or do something they wouldn't normally do. **71**

Bluetooth® A common short-range wireless technology, often used in PANs. **65**

Boolean A logical system using the operators OR, AND and NOT. Boolean data can take one of two values, either true or false.
  data type **8**
  logic gates **34-36**
  operators **16**
  symbols **36**

boundary data Test data on either side of the boundary of what the program should accept. **31**

brute force attack A network attack which uses software to crack security passwords through trial and error. **77**

bubble sort algorithm **5**

bus (CPU) A collection of wires that carry data, instructions and addresses between components of the CPU. **51**

bus topology A network topology in which all devices are connected to a single backbone cable. **67**

byte 8 bits. **37**

C

cache (CPU) Quick access memory inside the CPU. **51, 54**

cake **68**

Captain Firewall **72**

CAPTCHA Completely Automated Public Turing test to tell Computers and Humans Apart. Used to prevent software from automatically doing things like creating user accounts on a website. **72**

CASE statement A type of selection statement. **13**

casting A way of changing from one data type to another. **8**
  in Python® **23**

CAT 5e/6 cable Standards for copper Ethernet cables used on LANs. **66**

censorship The control (usually by a government or organisation) of what information other people can access. **76**

channel (Wi-Fi®) A small range of Wi-Fi® frequencies. **69**

character A single alphanumeric symbol. **43**
  data type **8**

character set A group of characters that a computer recognises from their binary representation. **43**

checksum A number used to check if a packet of data sent between networks has been received correctly. **68**

chillaxing **66**

clock (CPU) A part of the CPU that sends out a signal for instructions to synchronise to. **51**

clock speed The number of clock cycles per second. Determines the number of instructions a processor can carry out each second. Measured in Hertz (Hz) **51, 54**

cloud storage An online service where users can upload files to remote servers. **56, 75**

coaxial cable A type of copper cable with a low bandwidth but low cost. **66**

colour depth The number of bits used for each pixel in an image file. **44**

comment A note added to source code to say what part of a program does. **29**

comparison operator Compares two values and outputs either true or false. **9**
  in Python® **24**

Glossary and Index

Glossary and Index

Glossary and Index

Glossary and Index

storage device A device used to read and write data to a storage medium. **55, 56**

storage medium A thing that holds data. It can be part of the storage device (e.g. magnetic disks inside a hard drive) or separate (like a CD). **55, 56**

string A data type for text.
data type 8
in Python® 24
manipulation 11

structured programming A programming technique which breaks down the main program into small manageable modules. **29**

subroutine A set of code within a program that can be called at any time from the main program. **21, 22**
in Python® 27

surveillance The act of monitoring what people are accessing on the Internet. **76**

switch (network) Connects devices together on a LAN. **66**

syntax error An error in the code where the rules or grammar of the programming language have been broken. **31**

system cleanup utility A piece of system software that finds and removes files that are no longer in use. **59**

system software Software designed to run or maintain a computer system. **50, 57-59**

T

TCP (Transmission Control Protocol) A transport layer protocol that communicates with the recipient to ensure all data is sent correctly. **69**

TCP/IP model A network protocol model that separates protocols into four layers. **68**

terabyte 1000 gigabytes. **37**

terminator A piece of hardware used on a bus network that prevents data from bouncing back along the bus. **67**

tertiary storage High-capacity external storage used mainly for backups. **55**

test data Inputs that are chosen to see if a program is behaving as intended. **31**

testing A way of checking if a program functions correctly. **31**

test plan A detailed plan of how a program is going to be tested, including what test data will be used. **31**

time efficiency A measure of how 'quickly' an algorithm completes a task. **32**

topology (networks) How the devices in a network are connected together. **67**

trace table A table that keeps track of the value of certain variables as a program is run. **32**

traffic (networks) The amount of data travelling on a network. **69**

translator A program that allows source code to be understood and executed by the computer. **60**

transport layer One of the layers in the TCP/IP network protocol model. **68, 69**

trojans A type of malware which is disguised as legitimate software. **70**

trolling The act of trying to provoke public arguments online. **75**

truth table A table listing all possible binary inputs through a logic circuit, with the corresponding outputs. **34-36**

typical data Test data that simulates the inputs that users are likely to enter. **31**

U

UDP (User Datagram Protocol) A transport layer protocol that sends packets quickly without checking whether or not they are received. **69**

Unicode® A large character set that attempts to include all possible characters. **43**

units (of data) 37

user access levels Controls what files or areas of the network different groups of users can access. **72**

user account 58

user interface Provides a way for the user to interact with the computer. **57**

utility programs Software designed to help maintain a computer system. **59**

V

validation Checking that an input meets certain criteria. **30**

variable A named value which can be changed as the program is running. **10**
in Python® 23, 27
local / global 22

virtual server A software-based server. **78**

virus A type of malware which spreads by attaching itself to files. **70**

virus scanner A piece of system software that checks a computer for potential threats. **59**

volatile memory Memory that loses its contents when it has no power. **53**

Von Neumann A type of CPU architecture. **52**

W

WAN (Wide Area Network) A network which connects networks in different geographical locations. **65**

Waste Electric and Electronic Equipment (WEEE) directive 78

wearable technology Devices like fitness trackers and smart glasses that are designed to be worn while in use. **74**

well-maintained code Code that is easy for other programmers to understand and change. **29**

WHILE loop A type of indefinite iteration statement. **14**
in Python® 26

white box penetration testing A form of penetration testing where the tester is given system credentials. Used to simulate a cyber attack from within the organisation. **71**

Wi-Fi® The standard family of protocols used for WLANs. **66, 69**

WIMP A user interface based on windows, icons, menus and pointers. **57**

wired / wireless networks 65, 66

wireless access point (WAP) A piece of hardware that allows devices to connect wirelessly. **66**

WLAN (Wireless Local Area Network) A LAN that uses wireless technology to transmit data between devices. **66**

worms A type of malware which replicates itself. **70**

X

XOR A type of logic gate. **34-36**